The Grand Design - III
Reflections of a soul/oversoul

PADDY MCMAHON

Sooner or later questions such as "Who and/or what am I? Where did I come from? How can I find meaning in my life? How can I reduce the pain of self-realisation? What will happen to me when I die?" begin to niggle at each of us. This book provides answers that come from a spirit being named SHEBAKA.

The Grand Design books, of which there are five volumes, explore life in all its aspects both in the physical world and in spirit. Inter alia, they explain how we came to inhabit physical bodies and what happens to us when we die; and they provide facts, concepts and suggestions designed to help us, in cooperation with our guides/guardian angels if we so wish, to find ever increasing happiness and fulfilment in our expression.

CONTENTS

PREFACE

This is the third of a series of books which I'm writing, I believe, in association with a spirit being known to me as Shebaka. When I say the third of a series I'm not sure at this stage what that means in the context of whether there will be any more, or how many, more books in the series – although my feeling is that there will be two more and I've had a vision of the covers of them in particular colours.

As I'm writing this, it is May, 1992. Twenty chapters of this, the third, book have been completed. I feel an urge to stop and look at what it all means, or what I think it all means.

In my earlier life I never envisaged myself doing this sort of writing. I was always very interested in writing and tended to find myself in positions, in terms of career, where I had to do a lot of writing. I wanted more than that, though. Above all, I wanted to be a famous playwright – not just a playwright but a famous one!

I was born in July, 1933, in a rather remote part of County Clare, in Ireland. Stories of ghosts and fairies and the banshee (a female spirit who always seemed to be combing her hair and in attitudes of mourning – at least that was my understanding) were very much part of my childhood. There were fairy forts and pathways and bushes which were "out of bounds" for playing in, or walking on, or touching, or using in any way – all taken seriously (I think) by young and old alike, but mixed with orthodox Roman Catholicism in a curious blend of wonder dominated and limited by fear.

My mother was deeply religious and observant of all the rules and regulations to the best of her abilities. My father wasn't and, in fact, gave up the practice of religion altogether when I was still very young. (Whether a nervous breakdown contributed to that or not I don't know.) Images of a patriarchal, judgemental God and of eternal punishment through the indescribable tortures of Hell were given a more personal reality for me because of my constant fear that my father, whom I loved very much, would die without having had a chance to repent of his sins. When I was thirteen I went to boarding school, where there was a heavy emphasis on religion and the desirability of becoming priests. There were times when, in particular, the (to me) theatricality of being a priest appealed to me – the special clothes, the aura of mystery and of power, captive audiences, being called "Father" and treated with great respect – but really, I never had any intention of becoming a priest, in spite of the fact that I was very religious during my teens. While there was an ever present consciousness of the supernatural or the paranormal, there was a lot of fear associated with it – fear of punishment, hell, devils, spirits generally, and, in particular, evil spirits. I can't remember anything particularly unusual in a psychic context. I never saw any spirits – not even the banshee! The one thing out of the ordinary that stands out in my memory happened when I was 19. I had got a job in the Civil Service, in Dublin, in 1952. I had gone home to County Clare for the Christmas holidays. When I was leaving home to go back to Dublin my father went with me to where I was getting a bus. As he was saying goodbye to me I knew with an inner certainty that I wouldn't see him alive again – and I knew he knew. I resolved that I would write him a long letter saying all the things that I had never been able to say to him orally – at least, not since I was a child – but I hadn't done so by the time I got a telephone call, late in February, 1953, to tell me that he had died suddenly after a brief illness.

There was no obvious deathbed repentance as far as my father was concerned. I didn't, of course, want to believe, nor did I believe, that he could end up in a place of eternal punishment; but, in any case, I think I had begun to move away at that stage from the orthodox belief structure that I had grown up with and, if anything, my feelings surrounding my father's death accelerated that process rather than initiated it. From an early age I had been a voracious, if not a discriminating, reader and in my late teens and through my 20s and early 30s I was deeply interested and involved in theatre activities and did a lot of amateur acting and direction, all of which I practised and enjoyed for themselves, but, also, with the object of gaining experience to fulfil my ultimate aim of being a famous playwright. The exposure to a wide variety of ideas through reading generally and experience in the theatre clearly contributed to an opening up to thinking beyond the rather narrow confines of my own conditioning.

I got married, we had two children, I progressed in my career as a civil servant, my life fitted into fairly predictable routines, and I dabbled with writing plays, all the while telling myself that I would make a real go of it when I could retire from the Civil Service at 60. I managed to write a few plays and I entered them for occasional competitions and sent them to some theatre managements without success except to a limited extent in the case of one competition where my entry was considered meritorious enough to allow me to be considered for inclusion in a panel of writers for television. However, that, too, I put on the long finger waiting for the perceived paradise of retirement.

Then, in my early 40s, a new world opened up for me, which, as it evolved, made my ambition to become a playwright (even a famous one!) fade into the background and lose all its significance for me. Until I came to write this I had forgotten that a trigger point for me was seeing a book in a public library entitled "A World Beyond", by Ruth Montgomery. I borrowed the book and was fascinated by the scenario of life after death which it presented through communication received by Ruth Montgomery from Arthur Ford, who was well known as a medium during his earth life, from which he departed in 1971. Shortly after reading that book I heard about guides, which really turned life around, or upside down, (or downside up!) for me.

I had grown up with a strong belief in guardian angels. I found it a wonderfully comforting thing as a child. I used to talk to them then, but I don't remember ever having heard them talking back to me – just as well, probably, or I'd have been terrified, given the exposure to ghosts I was experiencing. But I thought of my guardian angels as my friends and there was no fear associated with them – as long as I couldn't see them or hear them! Later on, after my father died, I was terrified of seeing him, much as I loved him when he was in his physical body; such is the influence of conditioning.

Then, at the age of 44, early in 1978, I began to see and hear angels; a matter of fact statement which covers a plethora of mixed emotions. I was thrilled, intrigued, delighted, and, at the same time, disturbed. All the doubts and the fears of my conditioning came to the surface. Was it "good" or "bad"? Was I imagining it all? Was it the devil and all his cohorts of evil spirits playing tricks on me? Was I simply going mad? Walking along streets with people (in physical bodies!) all around me, I could hear other conversations in the air. Sitting in trains, I got visions of other civilisations and other ages. I looked at people sitting near me, chatting, reading newspapers or books, gazing out the windows, or just sitting silently, and I wondered about reality. Could they see any of what I was seeing? It didn't seem so. Were they the lucky ones to be unconscious of it all? Would I be better off if I could go back to being the way I was? I didn't want to be back there, but I found it very difficult to cope with ordinary, everyday life. I wanted to get away by myself to savour it all, and yet I felt I had to continue with my daily routines as if nothing was happening. I was abstracted and difficult to live with (more difficult than usual!). Yet, strangely, people I worked with didn't seem to notice anything unusual about me (I think!).

After a few months I realised that I couldn't go on living in what seemed like a multiplicity of worlds. Since I was on planet earth, I'd either have to leave it or be grounded in the experience of it. Then it came to me that the answer was simple – I could just ask my guides to control what was coming to me, to let it happen only by arrangement. I asked – and, miraculously, my life returned to "normal", or sort of normal. Perversely, I missed the excitement and wonder of all the continuing communication – but, at least, I was able to function within the physical reality of my environment.

Now, though externally life had settled back into some kind of normality, the internal change was enormous. Life had opened up into a vast vista of never-ending, evolving consciousness, which put all the happenings of day-to-day existence into a totally new perspective. And yet it wasn't new. Somewhere deep inside me I had known it all the time and the unfolding process as I began to write down what was coming to me became a joyful and wonderful journeying to the surface of my awareness. The name Shebaka didn't mean anything to me (other than that I liked the sound of it), which I found easier to accept – at the time I think I'd have found it very hard to accept a name that had historical associations for me. As it was, no preconceptions intruded on my consciousness.

As I said in the preface to the first volume, when I started writing I had no intention of publishing the material and even when I realised that what I was writing seemed to be assuming the form of a book, I thought that it would be nice and neat – and safe – if publication could be achieved posthumously. (I wasn't sure how I'd have managed that! Actually, though, I thought it would be a good test of the genuineness of the material if it was brought to public attention without my having anything to do with it.)

Again I'm repeating myself in saying that the writing has not been, in any sense, automatic. I am aware of Shebaka but not in a visual or obvious way. It's hard to explain; I can feel a presence and powerful energy flowing through me. Yet the energy is gentle and totally non-directive. I write in my own way and my own time and within the capacity of my own vocabulary and my own style. Ideas, concepts, facts are presented to me in a broad, yet unmistakable, way. I have to think a lot about some of them before I can put words on them, and sometimes I find it very difficult to express accurately in words what's emerging into my consciousness. More and more I'm being faced with the limitations of words and I can now see more clearly why complete, unambiguous, communication is virtually impossible to achieve verbally. Yet we have to deal in words within the restrictions of our earth existence, so it behoves us to do the best we can as we can.

The original title for the first book was – "Reflections Of A Soul/ Oversoul", which is now the subtitle. Later, "The Grand Design" suggested itself and, while it's not a particularly original title, it encapsulates what the material is about. Essentially, it aims to celebrate the existence of an infinite, all-comprehending, co-operative chain of love linking all souls together, yet with total respect for their individuality and free will, in a relearning, often painful, process of reaching back into a fullness of awareness lost so long ago by a small proportion (but a vast number) of all the souls in the universe. The first book gives details of the various states of evolutionary growth and, in general, is a combination of fact and philosophy. The second and third books are a continuation and elaboration of, and addition to, the material in the first.

The existence and availability of guides (guardian angels) to all of us is a central theme of the books. My childhood concept of guardian angels was of beings with wings under which I could shelter and let go of all my troubles. My present concept is fundamentally not much different except that I understand how guides have evolved to be what they are – and, of course, the wings are symbolical rather than real! My initial communication with guides was very obvious – as obvious, although not in terms of sound, as somebody talking to me. Then, as time went on, it became less and less obvious, so that I wondered whether it was all gone away, which left me feeling desolate and abandoned. But after a while I realised that I was being guided to see the communication as an integral part of myself rather than as something external to me, that I wasn't an automaton or a robot but, rather, an essential player (as everybody is) in the whole process of life and that part of my purpose in life was to show that there was no mystery about communication, that it was something that fitted into people's lives in the most natural possible ways without even having to think about it. I came to understand that what guides are aiming to achieve is to help us to reach more and more the fullness of our own potential without at the same time interfering with our free will, so that we always retain control of our own choices. It follows from that that guidance has to be unobtrusive and non-directive and is generally designed to help us find and benefit from opportunities for growth in line with our life purpose.

Something that caused me a lot of head-scratching, or soul-searching, or whatever is the appropriate expression, was the interaction of guides and what has come to be popularly called the higher self. That question is covered in the text of this book, but I thought it might be helpful if I highlighted it here because I have found it to be a source of confusion for a number of people. My understanding is that, for those of us who have not yet learned all that earth has to offer, our higher selves (or oversouls) are still some way short of regaining the ultimate state of full awareness. (The extent of the shortfall varies with each individual.) Accordingly, we are limiting ourselves if we seek to depend exclusively for guidance on our higher selves. Our purpose during earth lifetimes is to develop aspects of ourselves so that we add to the bank of consciousness which constitutes our higher selves (or oversouls). The grand design works in such a way that the oversoul sends out an aspect or aspects of itself in order to add to – or, more accurately, unveil (or unearth!) – its bank of consciousness. Until such time as it is safe to assume that the pattern of the soul's progress on earth is likely to continue to be in line with its life purpose, the oversoul plays a deliberately dormant role, so that if there is regression it will only affect the aspect, or aspects, which is, or are, temporarily going through an earth existence. With the help of its guides that aspect, or aspects, (the soul), will eventually (maybe through a number of lifetimes) progress to a stage where the oversoul can safely unite more and more with the soul, even while it is still on earth.

To sum it all up, then, the guides work in tandem with the oversoul to help it regain more fully its original state of total awareness. The guides have access to the totality of awareness/consciousness/all that is, which is not likely to be so in the case of the oversoul; but, even to put it like that is to create an unreal distinction since there is a unity of purpose between the guides and the oversoul and there is no need – indeed, it is irrelevant – to try to create a distinction. Each oversoul will eventually reach a stage where it will no longer need to be helped – but by then it will have long since developed beyond the need for earth existence.

In the first book, **The Grand Design – I.** the symbolism of the Father, Son and Holy Spirit is used, as follows:
Much of the teaching about God has centred on a divinity concentrated in three persons – Father, Son and Holy Spirit. As I have said, God cannot be identified in personal terms except in the sense that God is present in all persons. Therefore God cannot be confined to three persons unless they are seen as representing all life. I would suggest that it would be very

helpful to use the symbolism of the Father in terms of those souls who never lost or who have regained their self-awareness, the Son in terms of those souls who are still at the start of the journey or who have still not mastered the lessons of earth, and the Holy Spirit in terms of those souls who have evolved beyond the lessons of earth and who are helping others to find their way, for example, spiritual helpers or guides or guardian angels, whatever you wish to call them. In this way the chain of co-operation running through all life can be easily seen.

In another part of the same book meditation on unity with the Father is recommended **as a big help towards increasing self-awareness . . . . with the Father symbolising those souls who have never lost or who have regained their self-awareness. This is the ultimate goal which all must reach. If you meditate on it regularly you will find it a very rewarding experience. I suggest that you include your guides in the meditation so that it becomes a joint venture. Apart from the bonding effect, this will greatly help your self-awareness in your growth in self-awareness. If you want to verbalise in order to help your concentration you can use a form such as, "We and the Father are one" and let that serve as the basis of your meditation. After a while you won't need any words**.

I thought it desirable to include in the preface the above quotations from the first book since the symbolism is referred to in the text of this book.

In today's world the word "Father" has both a patriarchal and sexist connotation, but it is used in the books because it has traditional associations. If it is used in the suggested symbolical context the aim is that what was traditional will be seen in a new light and given new meaning, with meditation on unity with the Father bringing a feeling of merging with, (without loss of individuality), and being supported by, all the evolved energy of the universe. When we reach the stage of realisation (through feeling) of total unity with the Father (in the symbolic meaning given to the word), then we will **be** our fully aware higher selves or oversouls.

There is much emphasis in the books on how important it is to free ourselves from conditioned patterns of thought. Of course, we need to be able to think. It's wonderful that we can; how could we manage if we couldn't? Yet we are imprisoned by the effects of our environments, our cultures, our belief systems, on the way we think. How do we get out of our prisons? Obviously, it has to do with the way we think, the freedom, or lack of freedom, in our thinking. Can we analyse ourselves, think ourselves, out of our prisons? I don't think (!) so. I believe we have to let go of our thinking, judgemental processes altogether into the feeling of just **being** and, beyond that, into the feeling of unity with the evolved energy of the universe so that, eventually, we – once again – are that energy and we know that we are, without having to think about it. All that is explored in this book – particularly in the sessions entitled **Letting Go . . . Being Divine Consciousness . . . and Giving and Receiving Help: Expanding into Universal Love** but I wanted to highlight some of it, mainly because I have left the sessions in the date order in which they were written and I have made no attempt to bring them together by reference to subject matter and, conditioned as I am, I couldn't resist the temptation to try to put a shape on it all by saying what it means to me. At the same time, I realise that, in doing so, I'm attempting to put a shape on something which doesn't limit itself to shapes – which is why we find it so difficult to come to terms with the notion of God and, also, why understanding ourselves is such an apparently endless struggle.

It is noticeable in this book that there are long time gaps between some of the sessions. Once the first two books were written, and until they were both published, there didn't seem to be any urgency about getting on with this one. Anyway, I suppose, I hope, I was learning – or unlearning – more all the time.

Finally, I hope that any readers who have manifested themselves in female form in their present incarnations won't be offended by my use of "he" where "he/she" would be appropriate, but, in my view, too cumbersome for easy reading.

Paddy McMahon
May, 1992.

The final sessions in this book, on **unconditional love**, propose that growth in consciousness can be achieved through enjoyment rather than through suffering. I'm reminded that in the early stages of my communication with guides I was intrigued by the constant feeling of humour and joy coming from them. That seemed to be totally at odds with the concept of spirituality of my conditioning, which didn't seem to have much joy in it – indeed, a feeling of joy would have been a source of guilt, given that self-denial and penance paved the way to Heaven. So, after some time, I asked my guides how was it that there was always such a feeling of joy coming from them. The answer that came through to me, in a humorously direct way, was – "So you want us to be miserable!" And then it was explained to me that the essence of spirituality was joy, that the more true we are to ourselves the more we express joy; and in being more truly ourselves, the more centred we are in our own energy, and, of course, the more we can help others; if we're miserable, we only spread misery.

Paddy McMahon
January, 1993.

INTRODUCTION: GOD

30th October – 6th November, 1983: In our first two books, I have tried primarily to provide an understanding of the whole scheme of life with suggestions as to how to derive as much benefit as possible from life on earth.

In this book I propose to go deeper into areas already touched upon and also to explore new dimensions – that is, new dimensions in our communications although, of course, not new dimensions in themselves. Some of this material may be a bit difficult for you to absorb and to try. to put into words so don't be impatient if progress is slower than you'd like it to be. We will have plenty of time (in your terms) to record all the material that we have arranged to record – unless you fail to respond to the signals!

In your world at the present time there is a great emphasis on doom and gloom. And, indeed, in an earthly sense it is difficult not to be gloomy, Things like increasing unemployment, higher taxes, inflation, drug abuse, poverty, crime, hostility between nations and within nations, are all constantly brought to attention either through personal experience or through the media or both. To somebody who is unaware of, or cannot accept, the continuity of life the whole outlook must appear rather grim.

Side by side with these depressive elements, however, there are positive indicators of progress, even in human terms. For example, there is less world-wide discrimination than ever before, both racially and sexually; more attention is being focused on the unequal distribution of wealth and more attempts are being made to do something about it; society generally has become more egalitarian and less hypocritical in its attitudes; authoritarianism seems to have had its day – people are respected more for what they are than for the positions they hold; generally, there is more respect for the individual and for his right to live his life in his own way.

If the whole situation is looked at from an orthodox point of view it may be logical to conclude that the forces of good and evil have both gained and are gaining strength and seem to be heading for an inevitable confrontation.

There are, of course, more people now on earth than there ever were before. More and more souls are taking on physical bodies to try to speed up their spiritual development. This, as with any changing pattern, has inevitably caused disruption and an acceleration of trends towards harmony and disharmony.

I'd like to start this book on a positive note by a brief recapitulation of some earlier communications. Each soul is a part of God. Roughly 1% of souls lost awareness of this and what it means. The other 99% worked out a grand design of evolutionary growth to help the 1% regain their lost awareness. As souls evolve on their way back to full awareness they play their part in the implementation of the design. No soul, no happening, nothing at all, is overlooked within the framework of the design. Earth in all its aspects with all life on it is part of the design. Life on earth is a learning experience aimed at growth in awareness. Each soul has free will to choose how it will live its life. The grand design is infinitely flexible and adjusts itself to the vagaries of free will so that even if a soul regresses spiritually in a particular lifetime it will be provided with other learning opportunities to redress the balance and to resume its climb up the ladder of awareness. Each soul has, if it wishes, evolved souls available to it to guide it during a lifetime and to help it achieve whatever purpose it has planned to achieve in that lifetime. No soul can be lost because that would be negation of its nature as part of God. At the same time, many souls are experiencing a lot of pain and trauma in trying to regain their former awareness; and those souls who never lost or have already regained full awareness or are well on their way towards achieving that end are ceaselessly trying to reduce the pain and trauma while being very careful not to interfere in any way with individual free will.

The state of the world today, then, is a direct result of the operation of free will. But the grand design has kept on accommodating itself to that free will and there is certainly no danger of failure on the part of the design. The fact that unquestioning acceptance of traditional beliefs is no longer operative for many people has been seen by some as an indication of falling standards or decreasing virtue. It isn't so, of course. Spiritual progress is only possible for any individual when he questions his beliefs and establishes his own truth – which may or may not be in accordance with his beliefs. (I don't mean to imply that he should necessarily change his beliefs: what I'm stressing is that he should understand them and be in harmony with them for himself.) The possibilities for growth in awareness for mankind in general are now greater than they have ever been. Unfortunately, however, growth doesn't happen without turmoil of one kind or another. It is necessary to bear in mind that earth and the things of earth are ephemeral and are only of importance in so far as their spiritual effect is concerned.

Now I know you feel you've had enough introductory stuff and you're eager to get on to something new. So, let us begin, before we reach the limits of your patience!

I want to talk some more about the Source, or God, or love, or feeling and all its expressions, as I have described it earlier. You will remember that I said that all creation stemmed from feeling which defines itself in thought and that all this was a continuing process without beginning or end. Feeling is therefore the Source and all expression has evolved and continues to evolve out of it. Since feeling is constant and unchanging in itself – although continuously evolving in its expression of itself – it must always have been and continue to be. Where there is no such thing as time this is not such a difficult concept; think of a circle, which has no beginning or end, rather than a straight line, which has both.

I realise that, to somebody who is conditioned to believing in a personal God as the Source of all, the idea of the source being something as apparently nebulous as feeling may, on the face of it, be outrageous and sacrilegious. Yet God is often spoken of in orthodox teaching as being love, which can only be described as feeling and/or expression of feeling.

God or love or feeling expressed itself into individual souls. Each soul has its own style which gives it its individuality but the link of feeling or love binds all souls and all their creativity and acts of creation into one unlimited whole. Thus it is that no soul can indefinitely prevent itself from manifesting its true nature (feeling or love).

If feeling expresses itself in individual souls, and in individual persons in human terms, could there not be one Supreme Soul or Being or Person as the binding force? There could be in theory if that was the way feeling chose to express itself. But in reality it couldn't have so chosen; it would have been contrary to its nature, a diminution of feeling or love, to have expressed itself other than equally. The equality of all souls – no greater or lesser – is a fundamental characteristic of feeling, or love. As I explained in an earlier session, the fall from awareness of the 1% of souls happened because they were untrue to their own natures and sought predominance over their fellow-souls. Once there is a ruler – no matter how benevolent – and subjects, freedom is limited both for the ruler and the subjects. Feeling, or love, has to be perfect democracy if it is to be true to itself.

I have said that feeling is constant and unchanging in itself; when it expressed itself in individual souls did that not represent a change? It would have done had it expressed itself other than equally. But because it expressed itself equally there was no change in itself (its nature or style, if you like) – the change was only in the way it expressed itself.

Suppose, for the sake of illustration, that we look on feeling and individual souls as creator and creation and suppose that initially we narrow the idea of creator and creation down to a poet and the poetry he writes. Hasn't something been added, i.e., the poetry, to creation? If we broaden the idea, are all the individual souls not an extension of feeling and is there still a central feeling which is a constant although not manifesting itself as one Being? Central to these questions is whether creation is in essence separate from its creator. It is not and cannot be. While it is a fact that the poetry has been added to creation it is still a part of its creator, his expression of himself. Its essence is the feeling (which expresses itself in thought and then words) which went into its creation. This feeling cannot be something separate from the poet himself.

Two artists paint faithful reproductions of a particular landscape, yet the paintings will not make identical impressions on the viewers. What is it that makes the difference? Surely it is the feeling which is the essence of the creations (the paintings) which are themselves expressions of the artists.

Feeling is of its nature participative. If one part of itself had remained separate from its expression into individual souls the whole beautiful concept of equality and unlimited expression in accordance with absolute free will could not have been realised. There can only be said to be a central force or feeling in the sense that all are one.

Here I'd like to remind you of the symbolism which I used earlier of the Father representing all the souls who never lost or have regained full awareness, the Son representing those souls who have still not reached acceptance of themselves and their place in the whole scheme of things (who haven't progressed beyond the second stage of evolutionary growth as I have categorised the stages), and the Holy Spirit representing the souls who have evolved beyond the lessons of earth and are now helping others to reach their level before they themselves move on to the ultimate state. When this symbolism is used, unity with the Father, which means unity without loss of individuality, is the ideal for all souls, and help is constantly flowing from the Father in order to make that ideal a reality.

Before ending this session I think it may be helpful to record the following analogy. Think of the soul as an electric light bulb which is perfect but which is buried in earth. If the bulb were to be switched on it wouldn't show any light. However, when the earth is removed and the bulb is completely clean it shows all its light. Yet it is exactly the same bulb – perfect when buried in earth and perfect when the earth is removed. So it is with each soul. It will show its perfection when it sheds its unawareness, but the unawareness only clouds that perfection; it doesn't – cannot – destroy it.

Incidentally, in giving the example of an electric light bulb to illustrate a point, and in using words like perfection, I'm aware that I'm getting into limitations of structure. Perfection as a word implies a state where everything stops – no going beyond it. In the ultimate state of awareness there's no such thing as perfection in that sense – which would be very boring anyway, just stagnation; rather, it is a state of continually evolving consciousness. So the perfection which each soul will show as it sheds its unawareness will not be dull, or boring, or stagnant. It will be without limitation of any kind.

SOUL : OVERSOUL

2nd – 13th November. I don't want to have to keep on saying "as I explained earlier" or something like that, but as these sessions will be developing material already given as well as exploring other areas some repetition is necessary. In any case, it would be well that this book should stand on its own so that, while it would be desirable for readers to have read our earlier books, it shouldn't be too difficult for them to assimilate the material in this one without having read the first two.

Reincarnation, that is, repeated expression of a soul in physical bodies, is a fact of earth existence, which operates on the basis of a linear time sequence. The aim is to provide souls with as many opportunities as they need to enable them to reach a certain stage of awareness, or spiritual development. Life on earth can be very helpful towards that end, but souls are free to choose other ways also – instead of physical existence on earth – in which to learn the lessons they need to learn.

The needs of each soul are, of course, unique to itself. Initially all the souls (the 1%) who lost awareness went against their own natures and essentially no longer accepted themselves for what they were and are. So it can safely be said that, while the needs of each soul are unique to itself, all unaware souls suffer from a lack of self-acceptance. This has led to all sorts of negativities, for example, fears, anxieties, tensions, intemperance, intolerance, superiority and inferiority complexes, mental disturbance, bitterness, hatred, prejudice, greed, cruelty, disrespect for others, ill-humour, frustration, envy, diffidence, arrogance, narrow-mindedness, bigotry, fanaticism, power-hunger, lust, pride, resentment, possessiveness, aspects of which affect each unaware soul in varying degrees.

As a general rule, a soul in reincarnating into a particular body and environment is concerned with eliminating an aspect, or at most two or three aspects, of its negativity or, as I prefer to call it, its subconscious. The number of times it will choose to reincarnate depends on its progress in fulfilling its purpose during a lifetime as well as the extent of its subconscious or unawareness.

When a soul reaches the stage where it is ready to incarnate it is at least 50% conscious and certainly not more than 50% still subconscious. Its first incarnation will be aimed at reducing the subconscious by probably less and certainly not more than 1%. Thus it progresses – and sometimes, unfortunately, regresses – until eventually it is about 90% conscious, by which time it will have outgrown the lessons of earth and will not need to incarnate any more.

Because each soul has free will there was a risk that gains made in one lifetime would be counterbalanced in another unless life on earth was designed so as to ensure that the gains could not be minimised in any way. Accordingly, it was arranged under the grand design that the conscious mind would stay put, or dormant, and would only send out an aspect or aspects of itself during a particular lifetime. This is the concept of soul and oversoul which I discussed briefly in our second book. In this way there is a bank of positivity (conscious mind) which remains unimpaired no matter what may happen during a lifetime on earth.

An example may be helpful. An oversoul has reached a state of, say, 60% awareness (consciousness) with, accordingly, 40% unawareness (subconsciousness) to be eliminated. One of the aspects of unawareness which remains is bigotry. With the help of guides it chooses parents and an environment and designs a body and draws up a life plan to enable it to get rid of bigotry. The physical body of the baby which will accommodate the soul is constructed with its brain as the agent of the soul part of the mind (oversoul). Memory acts as a screen for the mind and only allows it to remember what it needs to remember in order to help it fulfil its life purpose. The soul has all the style and characteristics of the oversoul but its mental range is limited by its brain and memory. Both the memory and the brain operate in such a way that, in a manner of speaking, a spotlight is focused upon the aspects of the soul (feeling and thinking) which are orientated towards bigotry. While this is happening the other aspects (the oversoul) are dormant.

It's as if you are concentrating exclusively upon a particular task. While you are thus engaged you are only using a particular aspect of your mental faculties – in other words, you have far greater mental capacity than is needed for that task. If time stood still and you were "frozen" in the performance of the task, it would seen to an observer that you had no greater capacity than you were revealing in the performance of the task. That's what life on earth is like in spiritual terms.

The oversoul and the soul can be equated with you as you are and you frozen in the performance of a particular task. In reality there is no distinction between the two but I have used the terms in order to show that each soul/oversoul is a far greater being than is apparent from its physical manifestations on earth.

Soul (mind) is not a material substance and therefore the oversoul and soul are not like two separate bodies with one big one lying asleep while the other small one is out working. They are one whole but the major part of the whole is, as it were, playing a waiting game while the rest of it is developing itself. The development of the part will, of course, strengthen the whole – in other words, the mind will be freed of one more negative aspect (e.g., bigotry).

It is difficult for me to give an outline in human terms of the magnitude of the oversoul – a magnitude which continues to expand as the oversoul sheds its unawareness. However, you will get some idea of it if you imagine yourself with, say, the mental capacity to understand without effort all the philosophical concepts that have ever been felt or translated into thought or to call to mind without having to cope with memory all the poetry that has ever been created or to grasp immediately the most complex mathematical equations or to feel the loving and creative impulses of all souls spreading into yourself; in other words, if you see yourself as having an unlimited range of feeling and thought in whatever field you choose to interest yourself at any time.

The period of freezing, i.e., the period for which the soul is "away" from the oversoul, depends on how long it takes the soul to fulfil its purpose. It may be only one lifetime on earth, it may be several, it may be a combination of life on earth and life in spirit or it may be entirely worked out in spirit. It all depends on free will and how the individual soul responds to the help it is constantly being given. Then, when that purpose is fulfilled, another aspect may need to be put right; if that is so, another soul will, as it were, go out from the oversoul until it, in turn, fulfils its purpose; and so on until the oversoul reaches a state where no more than about 10% of its subconscious remains to be eliminated. At that stage there is no longer perceived to be any risk of regression and the oversoul brings its full capacity to bear on achieving the manifestation of itself in its former state of total awareness.

SOUL : OVERSOUL (CONTINUED)

16th – 27th November. Why wait until the oversoul is about 90% conscious before bringing it fully into play in the elimination of the subconscious? Well, I suppose the obvious answer is that the grand designers felt that there would be a risk of loss of some of what had been regained, that the 90% threshold represented the point of no return. At that stage there is no predominant aspect of unawareness left. For example, an oversoul might have some traces of intolerance and pride and power-hunger and perhaps other negativities but none of them would be present to any significant degree and they couldn't co-exist for long with the overwhelmingly stronger positivities. When I use a proportion of 90% I don't use it literally in the sense of clinical measurement; I merely want to show that there's a point at which all aspects of unawareness are reduced to such an extent that none of them is likely to gain any further strength at the expense of awareness already achieved.

I think that, for the present, we can leave aside the concept of soul and oversoul and I will use the term soul – or, I should say, I will revert to it – in talking about an individual being.

On the basis that many souls are still at a very low level of awareness and have a long way to go to reach even the second (human) stage, if a time measurement is applied, thousands of years, millions perhaps, are likely to have passed before the grand design is fully implemented. That this should be so is, of course, a matter of much regret and concern to all those souls who are aware enough to know about the grand design and its progress. However, they are encouraged by the fact that progress is being made, albeit slowly, and that there can be no doubt about the eventual outcome.

If the whole operation is going to take so long, does writing down all this material serve any real purpose? From an egotistical standpoint it certainly doesn't, but that would only apply to you personally. Who knows how many people may come to be helped by it? (There will certainly be enough time for that to happen!) Only about 10% of the people now on earth have asked guides to help them with life purposes designed in conjunction with the guides; but if each of those were to succeed in fulfilling his purpose the global progress, even in the brief duration of a lifetime, would be substantial. If some of the other 90% were to ask for guides to help them (and all they would have to do is express the wish; there are billions of evolved souls only too willing to help if asked to do so), the whole process of regaining awareness would be considerably accelerated.

In case of misunderstanding I must explain that evolved souls are helping all souls who have not yet reached their levels of awareness, but, generally speaking, this is not being done as a conscious two-way effort. Many souls have very definite ideas about what they want to do with their earth lives and they reincarnate with those ideas in mind. However, if they had asked evolved souls to help them design their lives on earth they would be likely to find that their ideas would have to be moderated or developed or perhaps discarded altogether if they wished to raise their awareness levels. On the other hand, many souls reincarnate with nothing definite in mind – they just want to be with a particular group, or they have got tired of life in spirit, or whatever. To a large extent they may be wasting opportunities for growth. What I am advocating is putting such opportunities to the best possible use with harmony of purpose – the more advanced helping the less advanced (teacher and pupil, parent and child, if you like) – in a progressive way.

AWARENESS V CONFORMITY

20th – 27th November. When a soul decides to reincarnate it automatically chooses to restrict the methods by which it can exercise free will. For a start, the pull of gravity on its physical body confines its freedom of movement. The combination of brain and memory restricts its freedom of feeling and thought. And the environment into which it chooses to be born conditions it further by its laws and general behavioural characteristics.

Many people rebel against the constraints. Some keep on moving from place to place in the hope that they will eventually find a community and a lifestyle that they feel will suit them. Some stay where they are but dissociate themselves from all communal activities. Some seek change by political methods or by using the communications media or by any other means open to them. Some break the laws and manage to do so with impunity or, if they get caught, are brought through the courts and fined or put in prison.

Most modern communities live under systems by which they periodically elect politicians as their representatives to govern them. The day to day business of state administration is conducted by public servants answerable to politicians, the representatives of the people. In-built into the systems are means by which existing laws are enforced – mainly through police, courts and prisons – and new laws are made. Thus it transpires that the individual member of a community, depending on his attitude, may consider himself to be protected or victimised by the laws and procedures made and enforced on behalf of the whole community.

What ought the attitude of the aware soul, or the soul seeking growth in awareness, be to governmental systems? They are unquestionably aids to spiritual development in that they provide many learning opportunities; for example, how to cope with power at the administering and receiving end; how to sit in judgement on the actions of others without also judging them; how to respect the rights of others to their own space and their own ways of thinking; how to overcome prejudice and bigotry and intolerance generally; how to learn to be mentally free in the midst of restrictions while at the same time not imposing in any way on the freedom of others; how to begin to see reality in the midst of illusion. The aware person recognises the systems for what they are – learning opportunities for spiritual growth – and uses them accordingly. He realises that by having decided to reincarnate he has chosen restriction of an obviously concentrated kind for the limited duration of a lifetime – restriction designed to produce greater freedom in the long run – and that there is no point in railing against the circumstances in which he finds himself if he considers that they are too constraining for him. What he does, ideally, is finds out what he has to learn from his physical conditions and then makes sure that he doesn't neglect the opportunities presented to him. By looking on the systems in this way he is not affected by them and doesn't take them too seriously. They are merely passing phases in history and have no importance in themselves; they are only important in so far as they serve as aids to spiritual growth.

Does this mean, then, that the aware person lives with the 'systems rather than seeks to change them? Not necessarily. Any change which will enable and encourage people to express themselves with greater individual freedom and to respect the rights of others to do so also aids the implementation of the grand design. It is of vital spiritual importance to each individual that he should learn to take responsibility for himself, that any institution (church or state) cannot do it for him. What I am talking about, of course, is spiritual responsibility, responsibility for what he feels and thinks, not material responsibility, which is of no ultimate significance in itself. Conservative paternalistic systems by their nature don't encourage individual freedom of expression nor consequently the development of spiritual responsibility. Accordingly, the aware person is likely to be a radical rather than a conservative, but he doesn't confuse radicalism with fanaticism or obsessionalism. He works to create, or to help to create, a climate of freedom of thought, but he doesn't fall into the trap of dogmatism, of thinking that his answers are exclusively the right ones. At the risk of being accused of being dogmatic I have to say that the aware person is never dogmatic! He may be firm in holding on to his own truths but in expressing them he is careful not to try to impose his way of thinking on anybody else.

THE FIRST STAGE: FURTHER ELABORATION

18th – 31st December: As I have categorised the stages of growth – or regaining of awareness – the souls at the first stage in earth terms are incorporated in the various forms, other than human, of non-stationary life. The difference between the first and second stages is that the soul has not reached a high enough level of awareness to enable it, in the opinion of the grand designers, to operate as an integrated entity with free will. Thus at the first stage one soul may be housed simultaneously in a multiplicity of bodies, e.g., insects, but this doesn't happen at the second stage – a soul uses only one human body at a time.

I have chosen to discuss this again because, while you take my word for it, you nevertheless find it a daunting and somewhat ridiculous idea that all sorts of fish and birds and animals and creepy crawly things are, in fact, souls. What idea would you find more acceptable? That all these creatures exist for no reason other than as a fact of nature? That they are there for the sustenance and use of humans? That they serve a mysterious divine purpose and that that is all you need to know about them?

There is no proof that I can now give you or anybody on earth that what I say is so is, in fact, so. All I can do is hope that my outline will prove acceptable to reason supported by observation of the orderly pattern of nature and non-human life on earth.

The strongest instinct in all living beings is that of survival. Some souls had become so fragmented and had reached such a low level of awareness that they had become almost totally unconscious (or subconscious) of themselves and of others – like, say, a person in a coma. The grand designers needed some ingredient which would rouse those souls from the apathy which seemed to have become their permanent condition. The creation of physical life in multiple specially-designed forms and the installation in those forms of brains with an overriding instinct for survival supplied that ingredient. In the spiritual sense survival is an unreal concept since non-survival is an impossibility. In the limited physical sense the implantation of an idea of survival spread through a multiplicity of brains is sufficient to bring about a consciousness of life and helps to encourage souls to continue the journey back to full awareness.

Evolved souls watch over all aspects of the grand design. It is difficult to conceive of a soul being temporarily fragmented into, say, a million fleas. Don't think of it as a physical concept; think of it rather as an attempt to spread consciousness. The physical vehicles are specially chosen by the evolved soul or guide whose responsibility that particular soul is, and the growth in the soul's level of consciousness is carefully monitored. At the insect stage survival is of paramount importance. At later stages the soul has more scope for self-development – for instance, in giving and receiving love.

I have already given my views on the eating of meat to the effect that if it is done with respect it is not a barrier to, and may help, growth in awareness. The grand design comprehends the killing and eating of one form of physical non-human being by another. While in physical terms this may seem to be barbaric it, in fact, strengthens the instinct for survival in both the killer and the killed. As the instinct for survival is sublimated or supplemented by development of other feelings the soul becomes more and more integrated so that at the second stage it is no longer fragmented. It is (usually) unthinkable for human beings that they should eat each other (physically!). It would, of course, be likely to be an interference with free will that this should happen. As free will is not operative at the first stage the killing and eating of non-human beings by human beings is not an interference with free will. However, if the killing is accomplished with cruelty – or is, for example, regarded as a sport – the awareness of the perpetrators may be adversely affected.

Is it a help towards increasing awareness to be vegetarian? It doesn't matter. In order to survive on earth it is necessary for a person to eat. What he eats comes from living physical substance and it is only the physical substance that's consumed. A soul cannot be eaten!

Many people are cruel to animals because they don't understand that they are also souls. Cruelty is often described as mindless; I can't think of a more apt description, given that mind is soul. Cruelty is a negation of soul to the extent that it obscures the loving nature of soul. I include all forms of cruelty, both physical and mental – although, of course, all cruelty is, in fact, mental. There are obvious forms of cruelty such as torture, or what are known as blood sports, but there are many less obvious ones, such as abandonment or neglect of dependent creatures; cruelty may often result from nothing more negative than mere thoughtlessness. Whatever about its manifestations or apparent consequences the perpetrator of cruelty ultimately causes most damage to himself, to his own awareness. Neither the hare which is pursued and mangled by dogs nor the dogs who do the pursuing and mangling are likely to be damaged to anything like the same extent as the organisers and participants in the event.

But what about animals which are commonly considered to be a source of infection or disease or, at least, uncleanliness, such as rats, or mice, or flies? Is it cruel to kill them? It's not possible to give a yes or no answer. It depends on the circumstances. In general, I think it best for a person's awareness that he should as far as possible avoid all forms of violence and treat all life with respect.

Many concerned people and many not so concerned people put animals down for one reason or another. Again, this is something which is best avoided, in my opinion. Animals are also working out their own life purpose, with guidance, under the grand design. They know instinctively when their time is up and they arrange their own going – if they are allowed to do so. It is difficult for a person to watch his beloved pet suffering, but that may be a valuable experience for both of them. From the spiritual point of view what's important is not what happens to the physical body but the effect that that happening produces on the mind.

Now you're worried about what you think is an apparent contradiction between my saying that the killing and eating of animals, if done with respect, is consistent with growth in spirituality, while at the same time the putting down of animals, even when done out of love and consideration for them, is not. Ideally, life on earth, including physical survival, is all one big co-operative effort designed to raise awareness all round. An animal whose physical body is killed and eaten is helping in that co-operative effort in the most basic way by contributing towards the physical survival of another or others. This cannot be said in the case of an animal which is put down. A person who takes an animal into his care becomes a partner with the evolved soul who has taken on responsibility for the soul which is temporarily and partly manifested physically in that animal. The animal's life is precious and its duration has been determined under the umbrella of the grand design by its guide. (Remember that free will is not yet operative in its case).

I don't want to say to anybody – in fact, it is not open to me to say to anybody – *This is what you must do, or this is what you mustn't do*. But, if I am to provide as helpful information as I can, I have to say that, in general, termination of physical life other than for survival purposes is not likely to be in accordance with the grand design.

But is it not an expression of deep love towards a distressed, terminally ill animal to have it put down to save it suffering? It may seem to be, but, in reality, (that is, spiritually,) it is a lack of awareness. Ask yourself – would you have a child put down in the same situation? If not, why not? The child is in your care also, is incapable of exercising free will as yet, and apparently doesn't understand its suffering any more than the animal. If you accept that they are both souls the parallel is exact.

Finally, how about the use of animals for experimental or research purposes in the interests of furthering scientific or medical knowledge? I think that the best way I can answer that question is by asking another -how would you feel about a child being used in that way?

PERSONAL INTERJECTION
(PADDY MCMAHON)

7th December 1992: The previous session was completed in December, 1983. Nine years later I'm writing this because of my own personal conflict over the death of a beloved cat, Wendy.

Wendy was a lovely tabby cat who came into our lives in 1980. She wasn't originally our cat but she quickly decided that she wanted to be, and, through a combination of circumstances, it became possible for her to come to live with us. She was a gentle, affectionate cat who never strayed far from home. By October, 1991, she was the only cat left in our household – one had died in 1990, and a second one, who was my daughter's special pet, died in October, 1991. So Wendy was on her own and when she seemed to have lost a lot of her playfulness and energy we thought at first that that was solely because she was grieving for the other cats. But, as time passed, it became obvious that she was ill. Eventually, we took her to our very understanding veterinary surgeon, who confirmed what we already knew, that she had internal tumours at an incurable stage. Having read 'The Grand Design – I' and having become very interested in the subject matter covered in it, he was slow to try to influence us in any way, while making it clear that he would be available at short notice should we need him – and, of course, we knew what he meant.

Wendy struggled on, but she was becoming more and more listless. She ate very little and movement became difficult for her. She was obviously most uncomfortable, even when she was lying down, or on my lap, which for a number of years had been a favourite place of hers (and, needless to say, that had made me feel good). How much pain she was suffering from, I don't know, but there was no doubt about her discomfort.

On 9th July we sent for the vet, on the basis that he would be coming to put her down. She seemed to know what was going on. She tottered over to where I was sitting and asked to come up on my lap. (She was no longer able to jump up.) I lifted her up as gently as I could and she settled down, putting her head into my hand, as she used often do. At one stage she turned to look separately and at length – apparently saying goodbye – at my wife and my son (my daughter was not present at the time). Soon – too soon. it seemed then – the vet arrived. She was lying on my lap with her back to him and she didn't turn to look at him – which was most unlike her. When he started to inject her with an anaesthetic she gave a plaintive little cry and jumped off my lap. He lifted her back up onto my lap but by then she was already nearly unconscious. He gave her the lethal injection and soon her little body was completely limp on my lap.

In agreeing to have Wendy put down (the words "put down" sound so harsh), I was conscious of what I had written in the December, 1983, session. Afterwards, I studied it again and "tuned in", thinking (hoping) that perhaps I had misinterpreted what had come through to me in 'the session. I didn't misinterpret it. So, since I have undertaken to record these sessions with all the integrity that I possess, I can't change the material around to suit my own situation. The only consolation I can give myself is that there are no absolutes, that each situation has to be taken on its own merits. Wendy wouldn't have been with us physically for much longer anyway. She was undoubtedly spared much discomfort by being assisted in her transition from the physical to the spirit state. What I didn't anticipate was that because her body died in a heavily drugged condition, she wasn't able to adjust naturally to her new state and, therefore, was confused for some time. I regret that very much, but I know that she's fine now and that she understands and forgives.

Through the experience with Wendy I now understand better the difficulties in adjustment which are caused for both humans and non-humans when they pass on while in heavily drugged and confused conditions.

NATURAL AND SUPERNATURAL

10th – 12th January, 1984: I hope that the people who read our books will come to realise that there's no great mystery about life after all. Many people live in fear of what they regard as the supernatural or the paranormal. This expresses itself in different ways, such as, fear of dying with all its attendant uncertainties, or fear of spirits, "evil" or otherwise. But, of course, since we are all spiritual beings, there is no death. It just so happens that some spiritual beings confine themselves in physical bodies for a time and while they are so confined their vision is limited by the density of the physical. When they leave their physical bodies behind ("die") they will again resume communication with souls who are still in spirit, or they may have to wait until those souls, or some of them, come back from an earthly trip. The only differences between spiritual beings – apart from individual style, personality, etc., – are in circumstances (such as having a physical body temporarily, or not) and awareness levels.

We are all supernatural or natural, paranormal or normal, whichever way you want to look at it. So there is no need to fear the "spirit world". No soul – whether in spirit or in a physical body – can influence you unless you allow it to do so. You are always in complete control of what you feel and think if you want to be. Once you accept that and apply it you are re-entering your own kingdom as a free spirit.

It may seem somewhat disappointing to think of spiritual beings in spirit as "ordinary" creatures such as spiritual beings in physical form (human beings) appear to be. In that context, I need only remind you of the soul/oversoul relationship which we discussed earlier. You may, perhaps find it helpful to think of the soul and oversoul as the natural and supernatural aspects of consciousness, respectively. So anybody who is afraid of the supernatural is really afraid of himself.

ANIMALS AND DEATH

12th January – 5th February: What happens to animals when they die? As we have seen, what appears in physical form as an animal incorporates only part of a soul (or mind). The first goal is the reunion of all the parts into one individual soul. (The second and ultimate goal is, of course, the regaining of full awareness by the soul.)

It may be helpful if we take an example of, say, a dog which becomes ill and dies. Its guide helps it through the transition in such a way that it is not, in fact, aware of the transition for some time – the equivalent of a day or so in your time. This period of rest (like sleep) is necessary so that the mental effects of the illness will be overcome. When it becomes conscious it is still in the etheric equivalent of its physical body but without infirmity of any kind. The first sensation it feels is hunger, and immediately a dish of its favourite food appears before it. The thought of the food produces it; the power of thought to actualise itself is much more obvious in spirit than it is on earth. (The power itself is not less on earth – its effects are less obvious.) Food is not necessary for survival in spirit and, of course, its substance is not material, but neither is the substance of the etheric body. What is produced as food can be just as real and as palatable to the etheric body as material food is to the physical body.

When its hunger is satisfied the dog's next thought is of its people, who are themselves also thinking of it and grieving over its passing. No sooner thought than done; the dog is immediately with them. They can feel its presence if they don't reason themselves out of the feeling or if they are aware enough to recognise it. It is possible for its guide to communicate with the dog in such a way that it realises that its people cannot see it and therefore cannot show their love for it in the same way as they did while it was in its physical body but that they still love it as much as ever.

It's a feature of life on earth that it's full of partings, in a physical sense, of one kind or another, the most notable being the death of the physical body. It's a great comfort to people if they can accept that these partings are not real; one soul is never more than a thought away from another.

To return to the dog; it stays with its people, or comes and goes to them, as long as both sides need the contact. At the same time it is being reintroduced to its other soul-part which had already completed a physical existence, also as a dog. (You will remember that in our first book I explained that according as souls progress through various forms of animal life fragmentation decreases until at the level of domestic animals it is likely to be limited to two or three simultaneous or nearly simultaneous physical manifestations.) One of the characteristics of domestic animals, which you may have noticed, is that they don't see themselves as being any different from human beings. Their awareness is sharpened by their contact with humans even to the extent of gauging their (the humans') often variable moods and accepting their behavioural inconsistencies.

In any event, the two dogs are placed in contact with each other for long periods by their guides. They become more and more attuned to each other's thought processes. They are being guided towards a merging of awareness or consciousness so that eventually they will become one integrated soul or mind. At that stage the re-integrated soul is ready to reassume the privilege (or burden!) of free will and to incarnate as a human being if it so wishes.

The same process happens in varying degrees with all other forms of animal life. When they pass on from their earth existence they are continually guided towards a merging of consciousness. The transition is slow; breaking down mental barriers always is. But it is a steady movement with all the patience and wisdom and support and love of myriads of evolved souls behind it.

SOUL : OVERSOUL (CONTINUED)

7th February: We have already discussed the soul in relation to the oversoul with the soul representing an aspect of the oversoul. If we accept that the soul incarnates or reincarnates manifesting a particular aspect of the oversoul, is it possible that a further aspect, or aspects, of the oversoul can be added during an earth lifetime? In other words, could the oversoul keep on manifesting itself more and more within the one body to the extent that at some stage it would be totally present within that body? Yes – but, in practice, only to a certain extent within the potential of one lifetime and the restrictions of one physical body. As you will have seen, what often appear to be sudden expansions of consciousness take place, sometimes rather dramatically, at different times in the lives of some people. New understanding dawns. Former ways of thinking and acting are discarded. People often wonder how could they have been like they were before, how could they have been so rigid, so intolerant, so narrow. The simple answer is that they are really different people or, perhaps, expanded people would be a better way of putting it.

If you remember, we discussed (in our second book and in this one) that when the oversoul sends out an aspect or aspects of itself (a soul) for growth purposes what remains behind is rather like a bank of consciousness. (At least, I hope that's a relatively simple way of explaining the concept of the oversoul.) According as the soul progresses positively on its earthly mission the way becomes clear for the oversoul to allow itself to manifest more and more fully on earth. However, in order to ensure that there is no diminution of the bank of consciousness already regained by the oversoul a further aspect, or aspects, of the oversoul will indeed, can – only manifest when the soul has already mastered its original mission. Needless to say, it would be – and of course, is – the ideal objective of each oversoul that it would regain as much as possible of its lost consciousness during the span of an earthly lifetime.

POSSESSION

12th May – 2nd June: Stories about people being possessed by spirits, particularly evil spirits, or devils, are as old as recorded memory. Through the ages it has been believed with different levels of intensity that such spirits often take over the bodies of human beings in pursuit of their own negative purposes.

I'm already on record (in our second book) as saying that it is not possible for any other soul to take over the body of a human being from the occupying soul. The design of the soul/body relationship is such that once the original occupant leaves it the body dies. When the soul travels while the body sleeps it does not sever its connection with the body; it remains connected to the body by what is biblically called the "silver cord" – which is essentially a connection of light. When the soul decides to leave the body ("dies") the connection is broken.

So what's to stop another spirit from getting into a body while the occupant is off on its travels and the body is asleep? The connection between the soul and the body is sensitive to any invading vibration (like a perfect burglar alarm!) and it is simply not possible for any other soul to take possession of the body while the connection remains unbroken. Could the other soul not break the connection and thus get in? No; once the connection is broken the body dies. This raises another question; are some deaths caused by invading souls trying to take over bodies? No; this possibility was foreseen when the grand design was being formulated. Such an arbitrary or random possibility would have introduced a measure of chance or accident into the implementation of the design and would have frustrated, or at least delayed, its fulfilment beyond the level of delay inevitably involved in the vagaries of free will; and, of course, it would be an interference with the free will of the original occupier of the body if the grand design allowed another soul to take over the body without the agreement of the occupier.

So we have established that a body cannot be taken over. But, of course, souls are free to exert influence in any way they wish. If you allow yourself to be influenced by another or others as to how you live your life, then you are, in a real sense, possessed by that person or persons to the extent that the influence controls your exercise of your free will. It is actually virtually impossible for a soul at the second stage of evolutionary growth to avoid being possessed to some extent in that development of consciousness either positively or negatively depends to a large extent on the interplay of relationships between souls. However, it is desirable that each soul should aim at consciously exercising freedom of choice in all circumstances. The more a soul grows in awareness the more it will try to help others to achieve that freedom.

But how can, say, an employee exercise freedom of choice in all circumstances since ultimately his employer tells him what to do? The employer tells him what to <u>do</u>, yes, and may even compel him to <u>do</u>, leaving him with the choice of doing or resigning from his job (which effectively may be no choice at all), but he (the employer) cannot control his (the employee's) feelings and thoughts; in other words the employee, if he so wishes, retains complete control over his own consciousness (what he is). Once he knows, accepts and applies that, he is as free from possession as it is possible to be within the constraints of life on earth.

The real difficulty with possession is that so many people want to be possessed. They wouldn't think of it in such stark terms, of course. They are looking for affection, for security or for direction so it often seems like a great help if somebody takes them over and nurtures them and tells them what to do. This whole area is a minefield; it is particularly so for those who are involved in any form of counselling. Rightly or wrongly, the counsellor is generally regarded as knowing more about such questions as how to be happy than the person being counselled. Because of this, counsellors may be tempted and pushed into positions where they may give directions to people who are only too happy to accept them. What are counsellors to do when people come to them in distressed states, not knowing what to do with their lives and looking for direction? It seems to me that the more aware counsellors are they can only take one approach if they are to be true to themselves; that is, to help people to find their own answers within themselves.

So where does this leave me with my constant emphasis on the desirability of seeking help from guides in all circumstances? Each soul is a universe in itself; it has everything within itself. When a soul asks its guide for help, that help is provided in a way which is consistent with the soul's purpose of reaching further into its consciousness of itself and what it is. Thus, a soul by seeking help from its guides is, in fact, tuning into its own higher self or consciousness and becoming more and more self-dependent or free of possession.

You may find it helpful to look at yourself in terms of how possessing or possessed you are by asking yourself such questions as:-

How much do you try to influence the behaviour of others towards conforming with your own ideas as to how they should behave?

How much do you allow your own feelings and thoughts to be influenced by others?

How free do you feel?

How accepting are you of everybody's right to exercise free will?

Do you expect somebody else to make you happy?

Do you regard yourself as the source of somebody else's happiness?

Do you consider that you have a duty/right to control another/others?

Do you see yourself as the moral guardian of another/others?

Do you use your position, e.g., of authority, to compel another/others to obey your will?

Do you manipulate another/others to do what you want them to do?

Do you send out negative thoughts, e.g., of bitterness, towards another/others?

Do you pray for another/others that he/she/they may, for example, behave in a manner which you think desirable?

As the questioning continues the thought will, no doubt, strike you that if you are to avoid possessing or being possessed you had better lock yourself up in a room and stay there without running the risk of communication with others; but even that could be a form of possession in your interrelationship with your immediate family or your friends! One can carry analysis to a point of absurdity. As you know, one of the big advantages of life on earth is that souls at different levels of awareness can interrelate unobtrusively because of the density of the physical vibration. In the interplay of relationships it is impossible to avoid influencing or being influenced, if only by example. So what I would suggest is that the simplest way out of the dilemma of possession is to bear in mind the special place that each soul has in the cosmic scheme of things and to respect each soul's right to fill that place according to its own truth. What you allow to others, of course, allow also to yourself. In loving yourself with all the tolerance and respect that that implies you arc freeing yourself to love others (all others).

TRANCE MEDIUMSHIP: GAMES

3rd – 5th June: It may be well to devote a little more time and space (!) to the subject of trance mediumship since you have been reading about it recently. You are somewhat troubled by an apparent contradiction between what is said (in our second book) to the effect that in trance mediumship the human's body is not taken over by a soul in spirit but that a form of self-hypnosis takes place and what you have heard and read about different trance mediums whose method of speaking, and appearance even, are often completely changed and who have no recollection of what transpired during a "performance". The word "performance" is actually a suitable word to use in this context because the medium is, in fact, putting on a show. The medium may be a retiring person or lacking in self-confidence or even somewhat doubtful or sceptical, but yet a person of sincerity and integrity who wishes to be of service to others; the trance method offers a neat solution la the dilemma of how to provide the service.

All human beings are actors. Life on earth is as much an illusion as life portrayed on a stage. The value of both is in their capacity to raise awareness. A play which is well-written, well-directed and well-performed will often have more impact than a conversation. People will tend to accept more readily information which seems to be more obviously coming from a disembodied spirit than an embodied one; even though the embodied one may claim to be receiving communication from a spirit source there is always the possibility for his audience that he is letting his imagination or his own personal views or interpretations take over. Elements of drama are incorporated (!) in a trance performance.

The grand design accommodates an infinite variety of methods of raising awareness. Souls in spirit and in physical bodies co-operate with each other in the implementation of the design. Trance mediumship is one form of expression of such co-operation.

It seems to me that, in general, human beings take themselves far too seriously. Life on earth is full of challenges, yes, or it wouldn't be of any value as a learning experience, but it was never intended to be a vale of tears. Today's crisis is usually gone by the time tomorrow becomes today. How well do you remember the happenings of last week, not to mention last month or last year? The game doesn't matter – it's how you play whatever game you choose that matters.

We seem to have moved from trance mediumship to playing games. Yet it's not really a move. All happenings are games. The only reality is consciousness. And consciousness in its aware state is joy, happiness, bliss, all included in love. Any game that helps people to realise that more fully is worth playing.

INDIVIDUAL RESPONSIBILITY

19th October, 1987: An appropriate subject with which to resume our sessions is, possibly, that of individual responsibility. To what extent are we responsible for ourselves? For our immediate families? For the cosmic pool of souls as a whole?

The central part played by free will in the spiritual scene is the most important factor in providing answers to these questions. All souls have complete free will with absolutely no restrictions. (How free will is exercised may lead to the imposition of restrictions, but that's a separate matter. Aware souls never interfere with the exercise of free will.)

It follows that as a spiritual being with total free will each soul must be fully responsible for itself. There can be no other answer. If any soul were to attempt to assume responsibility for another soul it would be interfering with that soul's free will.

There are certain circumstances in which physical responsibility has to be assumed – for instance, in the case of parents and children. The form of the responsibility could include caring, sheltering, feeding, clothing, etc. All this is usually done by agreement, as we have seen in earlier sessions. But it's a temporary arrangement which should not be allowed to obscure the fact that each soul has its own special, unique place in the cosmic design and that no other soul can fill that place or decide how it should be filled.

Our immediate families, of course, form part of the cosmic pool of souls. Once the question of physical responsibility is left out of the reckoning it is clear from what I have said above that each soul can only take responsibility for itself. It *cannot* deny any other soul the right to take responsibility for itself. It's not a matter of choice; the possibility doesn't exist within the expression of God/love.

My answers to the initial questions bring up other questions; for instance, am I preaching a doctrine of self-centred individualism? Where does loving, unselfish service to others fit in?

The fundamental prerequisite for any soul seeking self-realisation, including, of course, taking full responsibility for itself means that, ideally, it should never blame any other soul for whatever circumstances in which it may find itself. I don't mean articulating blame; I mean that no feeling involving blame exists. Paying lip service to this requirement or accepting it intellectually only is of no value spiritually; it's the feeling that matters.

If each soul, then, takes full responsibility for itself there are many effects; for instance, no grievances, no bitterness, no blaming, no dependence. No soul can achieve self-realisation for another soul. That's something that each soul must do for itself, although, of course, it may be helped if it is willing and able to receive help – which brings us to a second question.

There is often a lot of confusion about the notion of service to others, which springs mainly from a conflict between ideas of selfishness and unselfishness. At this stage it is advisable for me to define what I think are commonly construed as selfishness and unselfishness.

If a person thinks only of himself, does not in any way share with others of what he has, has no sympathy for others, never offers help, he is regarded as selfish.

On the other hand, a person is considered to be unselfish who always puts himself last, thinks of the needs of others before his own, shares with others of what he has, and is always prepared to help others no matter at what inconvenience to himself.

The question of motivation has, of course, to be considered where the unselfish person (as defined) is concerned. Why does he act as he does? Out of duty or love? Out of desire for reward (eternal) or recognition or with no such desire? Motivation is obviously a key factor in so far as the effects on his consciousness of his behaviour are concerned.

Each soul as love is a part of the whole cosmic love. Each soul, although it has its own individuality, is a part of every other soul. By developing its own awareness it also develops the cosmic awareness. The more it develops its awareness, the more its capacity to manifest itself as the love that it is grows. Love of its nature cannot be confined or limited. In other words, it cannot do other than share itself. The practical effect of this is that the aware soul cannot but be of service to others in whatever way it can. The only question, then, is what constitutes service or help.

I mentioned in an earlier session that help was continually flowing from the Father as part of the grand design. How much help is received depends on the readiness and willingness to receive help of those in need of help. The sacrosanct nature of free will is the key. You will remember that in our session on free will in our first book I used an example of a woman who seemed to be about to throw herself into a river. I put the question – do you stop her? And my answer was – no, if you are aware. I continued on to say that if she cried out for help then that was a different story. The point was that as an aware soul it was not open to you to interfere with her in the exercise of her free will, I deliberately used a stark example to emphasise the point.

The dilemma, then, for any human being seeking awareness is how to give help without interfering with the free will or the overall life purpose of any soul. Life on earth is so full of examples of people imposing themselves on others, or advising them in no uncertain terms what they should or should not do, or of people engaged in charitable activities, that it is difficult to be objective and to be free from the pressures of conformity.

Predictably, my best answer is that the more consciously a person works with guides the more he can be of service to others. Primarily, commitment is needed – commitment to allow oneself to be used as a channel of help, an instrument of love. This involves letting go of egotism which includes letting go of desire for recognition or eternal reward. Selfishness/unselfishness don't really figure in real service. One acts out of love in the only way one can act.

GOD/PERSONS, AVATARS, ETC.?

11th November – 21st December, 1988: "Go forth and multiply", "Teach all nations" – slogans such as these have been used throughout the centuries to encourage proselytism in one form or another. All sorts of methods have been used by people hell-bent (in a manner of speaking) on converting others to their beliefs. Although I used the expression 'hell-bent' jocosely, it is appropriate to bring hell into the equation because, in general, the most earnest proselytisers have been, and are, motivated by total sincerity of purpose aimed at saving souls from an eternity of punishment. The saving aspect is usually emphasised, and, more often, it is *saving from* rather than *saving for*; the eternal punishment is more easily conceived or imagined than the eternal reward.

As I mentioned earlier, when Jesus came on earth as Jesus he had reached the state of accepting himself for what he was – God, or son of God, if you like. He had accepted his own divinity, but not in an exclusive sense; he had also and equally accepted the divinity of all souls. He wanted to share his consciousness, to help others to reach the acceptance that he had reached. So, if being saved is defined as being helped to reach a total state of consciousness, Jesus can suitably be called a saviour – although I can tell you that he would much prefer to be seen as an example, or a guide, or a fellow-traveller, who had found out what direction to take to get out of the by-roads on to the main road and who wants to relieve all others of the pain of getting lost and/or coming to dead ends time and time again.

Are there specially chosen ones – god/persons, or avatars, or whatever else they may be called? As we have already seen, all are equal in God, or, put another way, God is equally in all. The only inequality is in awareness. Many souls of advanced awareness have come, and still come, on earth from time to time to try to help others. A common characteristic of all those souls is their true humility; they have come to an acceptance of themselves as God and all that that means and all that they are trying to do is to help all others find a similar acceptance for themselves. They do not look for devotion or worship or to be regarded as gurus; in other words, they don't set out to personalise themselves as God.

The various exhortations attributed to Jesus, such as, leaving father and mother and brother and sister for his sake, "Rise up and follow me" "Go, and sin no more", and statements, such as "I am the way, the life and the truth", are usually interpreted too literally. He was, of course, talking in a spiritual sense – pointing to himself as one who had achieved spiritual freedom or awareness and emphasising that this was the goal for everybody. He was drawing attention to the fact that in any relationship, no matter how intimate, it is necessary to achieve spiritual freedom (which may, or may not, mean physical separation). In our first book there is a statement in the session on freedom to the effect that a soul is what it thinks and that it can only achieve freedom in its thoughts. That is, of course, so; but, as we have seen subsequently, a soul is a combination of feelings and thoughts, with thought being a definition and articulation of feeling, so that, when we talk of spiritual freedom, we can go a stage further and see it as a totality of expression through feelings and thoughts. You are a spirit being, an expression of God, creator and created, what is and all that is, individual consciousness and collective consciousness, limited awareness (temporarily) and unlimited awareness. A soul will never be able to reach full awareness until it accepts completely all that is expressed in the last sentence above. Acceptance involves understanding, knowing, that what is so for one soul is also so for each and every soul without exception. Such acceptance has all sorts of implications, e.g., non-interference with free will, making no judgements, non-possessiveness. What a soul accepts for itself it accepts for each and every other soul. It follows that there is no dependency, in a spiritual sense, no attachment except in a loving way, letting go, setting free. There are no hooks, no chains, in spiritual freedom.

LETTING GO

31st December, 1988 – 18th January, 1989: Now that we have reached another year in terms of your time scale it is, perhaps, appropriate to discuss what I would like to call a "letting-go" process. Within the physical earth framework one can't hold on to time. Day follows day, week follows week, month follows month, and year follows year relentlessly and inescapably. So a soul living within a physical body has to let go of each day, week, month, year. The trouble is that letting go, not just of time but of all the happenings, etc., during the passage of time, can be painful. Lost: youth, looks, virility, agility, sporting ability, opportunities for creative expression, remunerative employment, child-bearing, etc.; physical faculties, such as, sight, hearing; parents, children, spouses, relatives, friends, lovers, are but some examples of sources of pain which seem to be inseparable from the earth experience. Given that time does not stop, neither can the process of ageing, with all its physical implications, nor separation, with all its pain of loss. So how does one lessen the pain – or, better still, find freedom from it altogether?

We have now come to a question which is central to the whole purpose of life on earth.

Clearly, the grand design comprehended that human beings would become attached to each other and to many of the things, activities and attitudes which are inherent in the earth experience, for example, food, drink, sex, clothes, gambling, reading, writing, painting, sculpting, sports, drugs, business, politics, conflict, religion, power, authority, making money, status, competition, illness, grievances, beauty, piety, duty, righteousness, judgement, sarcasm, morbidity, joylessness, inferiority and superiority complexes, and so on. The grand design also obviously envisaged that sooner or later detachment, non-attachment, would occur. Death of the body provides an enforced physical separation. This is intended to point the way towards detachment, or, as I prefer to call it, non-attachment. Life goes on (to coin a phrase!). People have to continue to cope with the daily challenges somehow without the physical presence of their loved ones. They have had to let go physically. If they can let go mentally *while continuing to love* then they are on the way towards accepting that they themselves are free spirits and, most important, that so, too, are all others.

In my view, letting go is a process of becoming, which sounds like a self-contradictory statement to make. In the interest of simplicity I'll use a personal approach. You believe that you are divine consciousness. You have not yet acquired the totality of that consciousness (or regained it, I should say) – you are still rubbing off the earth of unawareness. Negativity does not – cannot – co-exist with divinity. Therefore, the more aware you become the more you let go. For example, if you are worrying about how you are going to find enough money to pay the electricity bill, you let go of the worry into the knowledge that divine consciousness never worries about anything and that the means of paying the bill will be present for you when needed.

Incidentally, there is a certain conditioning and, consequently, security about worrying. People are often considered to be lacking in feeling if they don't worry. An expected response is, or becomes, a form of security. Of course, worry is not alone a waste of energy but, even worse, is a pressurising thought form on the object of worry.

Divine consciousness does not need anything. There's no pain of loss because there is no loss. There's no pain of separation because there is no separation. When I talk of letting go I mean *letting go of unawareness into awareness*. The fundamental and essential starting point is acceptance that you and all souls are divine consciousness. Letting go of all fear into that consciousness follows in due course. Until it does, you have not yet reached full acceptance of your divinity. Belief is not enough; it's an intellectual exercise only. Acceptance is totally spiritual; it is harmony of feeling and thought into consciousness.

BEING DIVINE CONSCIOUSNESS

11th February – 21st February: We have talked about each soul having God within, or, in other words, being love or divine consciousness. Assuming that you have no difficulty accepting that, either through your thoughts or your feelings, how do you contact the God within and thus be consciously divine while still also human? For a start, I suggest that you remind yourself constantly that you are divine consciousness temporarily using a physical framework. The more fully you accept that, the more you will manifest it without separation into a duality of human and divine or material and spiritual. Accordingly, essentially there shouldn't be any question of contacting the God within, which implies separation, but, rather, of allowing yourself to be God, which means integration. That's easier said than done, of course, especially when you are faced with physical problems, such as illness, or relationship or financial difficulties. In such circumstances how do you actually manifest your divinity? Suppose you say to yourself – 'I am God', or, 'I am love', or, 'I am divine consciousness', and – 'God/love/divine consciousness does not have problems or difficulties', what process should take place? Do you work through your feelings or your thoughts, or both, or do you see yourself as a spark or an expression of divinity letting go into the wholeness of divinity, or what?

May I remind you of the meditation I suggested in our first book about being one with the Father, with the Father representing all the souls (the 99%) who had never lost awareness. This is a sweeping concept which in the human condition is difficult to imagine – rather like statements such as – 'All is one', 'One is all' – so let's try and break it down a little. You are an individual soul and so is each and every soul. Yet, in a state of full awareness you are also one with each and every other soul and with all life. In terms of consciousness you are your own consciousness but you are also linked to the universal consciousness – like a wave in the sea. The wave has all the qualities of the sea and is the sea but is not all the sea – yet it is all in the sense that it is inseparable from the sea and is in unity with it. (The sea, like the example of a jig-saw puzzle, is a limited analogy in that God is more than the sum of all the parts, as I explained in our earlier books.)

So where are we? God is within you. You are, in fact, God (or love), but that's obviously not an exclusive proposition since each other soul is also God. In contacting God, accordingly, does that mean that you contact all consciousness, aware and at varying levels of unawareness? It could mean that, and that's why I suggested meditating on unity with the Father so that then you are merging with full awareness. Ultimately, of course, there will again be a unity of total awareness when all the souls still searching have found their way back to full awareness.

Now we come back to the method. Do you have to have an image in your mind before you can meditate? For instance, is it helpful to personalise the Father, or use symbolism, such as the wave and the sea? In my view, using the symbolism would be a better approach than personalisation since personalisation intrudes a sense of separation and limitation. If a feeling of unity can be achieved without either personalisation or symbolism, then that's the best way. Once you inject an image, whether a personalisation or a symbolism, you are starting with an intellectualisation, from the outside in, rather than from the inside out. As I explained in our second book, the source is feeling (love). Feeling is being. Feeling expresses itself into thought in the ideal balance of being. So, in my view, the best way to contact the God within is to let go of all thought as far as possible and simply to be, to let the love that you are take over. You can describe, rationalise, define through thought but you cannot think yourself into being. The being (feeling) comes first before the thought.

Suppose you are feeling happy. You start thinking about why you are happy. Then you have lost the *feeling* of happiness. You have circumscribed it, analysed it and changed it. Or you are listening to music, absorbing it into your being. You begin to wonder what is it, who composed it, etc. Again, you are now limiting the feeling. Or you are walking, feeling the peace of a quiet countryside. You start observing wild flowers, categorising them, or trees, or whatever; once again you are channelling your feelings into a thought process of definition which may very well be enjoyable but is nonetheless a separation from the feeling of integration with the countryside.

You are conditioned by thought patterns. Your conditioning predisposes you to slot everything into patterns of what you know. Thus you constantly limit yourself. How do you know you have a problem? Because thought tells you so in its analytical, judgemental functioning. How to change that? You are faced with a situation which thought tells you (from its conditioning) is a problem. Suppose you are married, the sole breadwinner of a family of five, with a heavily-mortgaged house, but with a level of salary which enables you and your family to enjoy a comfortable standard of living. You lose your job and have no immediate prospect of getting another one. The process of thought tells you that if you cannot get a job with relatively the same level of pay as your previous one the standard of living of yourself and your family will have to be reduced considerably, not to mention the fact that your house will probably be repossessed by the financial institution which made the mortgage arrangement with you. No matter how you think about it, the answer is still the same – get a new, equally well paid job, or accept a drastically-reduced standard of living. Thought puts you into a strait-jacket of options.

So here is a concrete situation to put the question of contacting the God within to the test. My way of dealing with it would be to stop thinking about it altogether and hand it over to the divine consciousness which you are. Divine consciousness (God, love) will present a solution to you – which will lead you into a new and expanded pattern of thought – if you let it. That sounds passive but, in reality, it means that the energy of all evolved souls will be channelled by your guides into solving your difficulty.

You are still somewhat puzzled about the method of contacting the God within or handing over to your divine consciousness. The difficulty is in trying to rationalise something which cannot be rationalised. So now you have created a problem for yourself. Stop thinking about the how and let go into the feeling of being love. Then you are at one with the God within and the question of making contact no longer arises.

But, you ask, in order to let go, don't I have to think about letting go? So doesn't the process start with thought if only on the basis of thinking not to think? Ideally, feeling and thought are totally harmonious functions of mind (soul) and, accordingly, are not separate from each other. They only become separate when thought defines feeling in terms of conditioning. Suppose we look again at the situation of the person who lost his job. His conditioning influences his thinking in certain directions. Until he stops thinking about his problem he is restricting the possibilities of solving it into the limitations of his own thought patterns, influenced as they are by his subconscious mind. When he lets go into divine consciousness he allows himself to be free of his subconscious so that his feelings and thoughts can work in harmony, united in consciousness.

Words are an inadequate form of communication in this area because by their nature they define and, therefore, limit. I don't use words – as you know them – any longer as a means of communication. That's why this has been such a difficult session for you, since you have to deal in words. However, we have done our best.

HOW TO BECOME MORE CLAIRVOYANT/CLAIRAUDIENT

2nd – 3rd March: How can one become more clairvoyant or clairaudient in other words, break down the barriers between what are classified as the natural and supernatural? We have looked at this earlier in talking about communication with guides. I'd like to go into the subject in more detail in this session.

The following are my suggestions:
1. Ask for guidance.
2. Get yourself into as relaxed a position as possible by whatever method suits you.
3. Let yourself go mentally limp – in other words, suspend thought – as far as you can.
4. Press briefly and occasionally your right thumb into your throat just below the corner of your jaw. This is an aid towards clairaudience.
5. Massage slowly and gently, again with your right thumb, the third eye area in the middle of the forehead in an anti-clockwise direction for about two to three minutes a day. This helps clairvoyance.
6. Bear in mind that communication is a continuing process and that one doesn't have to wait for "a flash of lightning"; once you consciously tune in, the insights that come to you are likely to be valuable.
7. Don't let yourself be pressurised by the passage of time; silence may be exactly what's needed in a particular situation, so if you have a blank, don't worry about it.
8. Communication is easier if you have specific questions as long as you free yourself from commitment to a particular answer (which might be likely to confuse your communication).

9. Don't seek to give directions or to control. Aware guidance is always given in a non-directive way so that free will is never imposed upon. The central purpose of this type of communication is to increase awareness, not to encourage the generation of robots.

10. Don't make any judgements. Remember that there are no absolutes. Judging is an ego trip and is likely to follow the pattern of your own conditioning.

11. Bear in mind that communication between the non-physical and physical worlds is normal rather than abnormal but that there are difficulties related to time and space which are a feature of earth life only; so don't adopt black and white standards or take too literally what you're given.

12. Trust your imagination, especially when you're in a relaxed frame of mind. Once you have asked your guides not to let negative influences come through to you, your imagination will provide the answers you need.

13. Good communication is not a matter of technique but rather of relaxation, patience, trust, commitment, honesty, open-mindedness, tolerance, freedom from conditioning, respect for each soul's privacy and free will, and, above all, expanding love.

Communication with guides is not designed to be straightforward in the sense of the guides doing all the work; otherwise there would be little or no growth for the human communicator. Ideally, as communication develops it is difficult to distinguish between what's coming from guides and what's in the mind of the human agent; the human and non-human (spirit) merge in an integrity of communication. Thus the human is never just a channel. All his previous experience, through countless centuries in terms of earth time, has brought him to a level of awareness which he now shares with others, while at the same time he leaves himself open to inspiration which is flowing to him from his spirit helpers. All through history the people who have helped to raise awareness have been able to do so because they consciously or unconsciously left themselves open to inspiration. That in no way diminishes them; rather the reverse, since they reached out beyond the limits of the physical framework to tap into the universal consciousness. Even though we are, each, individual, yet we are all one, so that my contribution to the universal consciousness is equally yours as yours is mine. That's why it is so important that each soul finds its way back to full awareness; in doing so, it automatically helps every other soul.

CATEGORISATION: SCHIZOPHRENIA

24th March – 24th May: You have been reading about enneagrams and fitting into personality-type categories. Each soul chooses to operate primarily through certain qualities which have both positive and negative aspects depending on how well-balanced or unbalanced the soul is. However, because of an over-emphasis on a rational or scientific approach there has been a prevailing tendency to try to put people into boxes or types. This makes for neatness, security, it puts a recognisable shape on the world and everything in it. It is an understandable approach because everything in the physical world has a shape and since the process of thought tends to be conditioned by experience it only knows shapes and, therefore, limits. What I'm saying, then, is that categorisation equals limitation and ultimately needs to be avoided. It is essentially making judgements.

But surely judgements have to be made in some instances? For example, take the mental condition known as schizophrenia; mustn't it be conceded that certain people at certain times are schizophrenic? And if that is not acknowledged how can they be healed? Schizophrenia is indeed a suitable example because it illustrates the human condition. The earth experience was designed because souls had separated themselves from their own divinity. All souls on earth, then, are to a greater or lesser extent separated from their true selves and are trying to regain their former integration. In its ultimate state of awareness each soul has all the qualities of the whole (God) while retaining its own individual style of expression – which is what makes it individual. What you call schizophrenia is a more extreme form of the separation which is a feature of humanity.

For developmental purposes it can be useful to highlight the fact that individuals may have chosen to come on earth with an emphasis on certain qualities more than others – in other words, they can fit into certain personality types. Undue highlighting of those qualities may, however, be detrimental to a person's ultimate growth since the aim is to achieve total integration of self as far as possible, which means that as a person develops it becomes increasingly difficult to fit him into any category or personality type.

Now I'd like to discuss schizophrenia since in many ways it may be the best example of categorisation. If you look up the word 'schizophrenia' in your dictionary you will probably find it defined as a mental disorder leading to irrationality, delusions, split personality, or something like that. In my view, medical science hasn't even begun to reach an understanding of the condition and will continue to fail to do so as long as it approaches it in a scientific way.

Being born into a human body is a severe and traumatic adjustment for every soul. Imagine yourself as: a bird which can't fly; or as a prisoner locked indefinitely into a cell where you have room only to stand in a crouch or lie down doubled up; or as an avid reader trapped in a long-term situation where you have no access to books; or as a musician who has no hope of finding an instrument on which to play; or as a hopelessly disabled person who can't move; or in any extremely restricting situation, and you will have some idea of what confining the soul within a human body means. Is it any wonder that the body was designed needing sleep so that the soul would have an opportunity to "spread its wings" (in a manner of speaking!) at regular, not too far apart, intervals?

Even though each soul has a free choice as to whether it will incarnate or reincarnate in a human body, in the case of some souls, circumstances (the effects of their accumulated experiences on their consciousness) have combined to make it highly desirable that they should attempt the balancing challenge of earth. At the same time, they know what a struggle it's going to be. They know that temporarily they may, through the use of their free will, make things worse rather than better. So it is hardly surprising that they often come in red-faced and screaming. (It's thousands of times worse that the Monday morning feeling so many people have to endure.)

The whole point of the earth experience is, as we have discussed earlier, to help souls regain their former integration. If they can get a sense of that integration, even some feeling of it, within the harshly separating conditions of earth, then they will have achieved a great deal. Fundamentally, it is ultimately essential that no separation should be felt between God and man, soul and body, spiritual and material or physical. The trouble is that people, through conditioning or otherwise, tend to reinforce the separation; for example, God is seen as a powerful, often threatening, separate Being; to be spiritual one has to reject the material, including sometimes one's own body; there's no proof that there's anything beyond the physical so if one wants to be obsessive about alcohol, or drugs, or sex, or making money, or any other physical activity, then why not?; and so on. Obsessiveness (which, of course, is often religiously – as distinct from spiritually – orientated, too) tends to be a reaction, or, more accurately, an overreaction, to the conflict inherent in the soul's reluctance, yet choice freely made, to come on earth. The schizophrenic soul knows, probably unconsciously, that it needs to be on earth, but cannot adjust itself to the restrictions involved. On the one hand, it rejects its body and, on the other hand, seeks to over-identify with it, for example, by excessive indulgence in sex, or drugs, or alcohol, or food.

The difficulty for psychiatrists, psychologists, psychotherapists, or any others who work in what I might generally label as a counselling field, is that, wonderfully motivated people though they usually are, they may not fully understand and/or accept who and what they themselves are. ("Physician, heal thyself" takes on a new meaning in that context.) If they don't, how can they help a more obviously separated personality to integrate itself? Integrate itself into what? The best they can hope for is to help it to conform with what are regarded as the normal standards of society, somebody who "fits in".

The history of humanity shows that throughout the centuries human beings have tended to organise themselves into groups, such as, political parties, religious organisations, societies and clubs of various kinds. Each group formulates its own rules of membership and creates its own power structure. A network of security and belonging is thus provided for the individual member, with, also, in some cases a fanatical or obsessive sense of purpose. A common tendency in the groupings is to be protective of their members and ruthless towards those who fall out of line or break the rules, although, depending on the climate of the times, the ruthlessness may seek to be cloaked in a veneer of civilised concern. A person who does not belong to a grouping of some kind is likely to be, or to feel, isolated in some way, or else to seek to create his own sense of status by being deliberately "odd", or radically individualistic.

In my view, because of the human addictiveness to power, status and exclusiveness, all organisations, *without exception*, are potential vehicles for the reinforcement of schizophrenia or separation. Symptoms, such as unpredictability of behaviour, tend to manifest themselves more obviously in those who somehow feel pressurised or isolated by the grouping in which they find themselves.

So what's the best way to deal with schizophrenia or any kind of mental imbalance? Initially, I suggest that all those who are involved in mental treatment (e.g., psychiatrists, psychologists, psychotherapists, counsellors) should integrate themselves as far as possible, if they have not already done so. By that I don't mean that they have to be perfect; indeed, rather the reverse, since the more they understand and accept their place in the grand design, the more the burden of perfection will fall away and they will realise that they are always in a state of becoming. In any case, it would be impossible for their clients to identify with them if they were perceived as perfect! I have already explained (too often, perhaps) what I mean by integration, so I won't go into it again now. Once they have dealt with themselves, they know at least what's wrong with their clients and they are treating fundamental causes rather than symptoms. The emphasis in their training on being non-judgemental is of great value. (But how well do they apply that to themselves in their own personal lives?)

The spotlight is now focused on the client. For ease of reference, I'll call him James. The game of life on earth has become too much of a burden for him – unfortunately, he doesn't see it as a game – so somehow he has to be encouraged to start again, but with a different foundation this time. This means that, in effect, he has to become a child again.

A child sees, touches, tastes, and, above all, feels and expresses its feelings. The process of thought is largely suspended. In James's case, (as, indeed, in all similar cases) his thought formation has become a victim of his subconscious, so he needs to be helped to create new patterns of thought.

The treatment I would recommend for James, then, is that he identify with everybody and everything within his range of experience from the fresh perspective of a child. This would mean that even with members of his own family he would seek to shed all his preconceptions and look, listen, touch, taste and smell with new eyes, ears, hands, mouth and nose. It would be desirable that he should avoid categorisation. Seeking to identify things (and people) by description creates a separation from them. For example, if James sees a tree he can better identify with it if he doesn't seek to categorise it as ash, beech, etc.; or, if he is listening to music, he separates himself from the sound and harmony and feeling of it if he starts trying to remember its title and who composed it; or, when he meets people, it's much easier to relate to them if he doesn't compartmentalise them, e.g., well-dressed, crooked nose, black, white, fat, thin, and thus form snap judgements about them which emphasise his separation from them.

Certain questions ask themselves, e.g., how can James be induced to adopt the approach outlined above and, if he does, how can he survive in the everyday world without appearing to be a simpleton who knows nothing about anything? He is a free spirit, an indispensable part of divine consciousness, and it would be an interference with that freedom if he were forced to undergo treatment. Given that he recognises that he needs help and is prepared to receive it, it would be ideal if treatment could take place in an environment where he would be temporarily free from ordinary day to day pressures and where there would be complete understanding of the process being undergone by him. In a manner of speaking, he has been reborn and the adults around him need to treat him as they would a child.

In my opinion, all forms of mental illness are due to extreme egocentricity; in other words, concentration on the narrow, limited "i", rather than on the universal, unlimited "I". So the ultimate answer is to make the jump from the limited to the unlimited. The jump is a risky one if neither the therapist nor the client has a clear understanding of the unlimited "I".

GIVING AND RECEIVING HELP;
EXPANDING INTO UNIVERSAL LOVE

25th May – 29th May: What can you do, though, if somebody does not recognise that he needs help and yet is obviously in a divided or schizoid state of mind? Primarily, I recommend that you project loving feelings and thoughts towards him. But I would like to develop that answer into a general suggestion regarding giving and receiving help and expanding into universal love.

Stand as still as you can and allow yourself to feel that your guides are forming a circle with you. Let yourself relax into feeling: – love flowing round the circle; that the guides are channelling into the circle all the evolved energy of the universe, of God, of which you are essentially a part and which is, of course, in you; that you are accepted and loved totally as you are, without having to put on an act of any kind, and that that love is constant, unchanging, non-judgemental, unconditional: that whatever burdens may be on you – fears, anxieties, tensions, stresses, worries. pressures of any kind – are lifted from you and the universal love is taking care of them; that the universal love is enabling the total fulfilment of your life purpose so that whatever opportunities you need are manifesting for you, and will manifest for you, in the best possible ways at the best possible times; that you are expanding into, and at one with, the universal, unconditional, love; that you are secure in the feeling of being always guided and protected and loved in a way that's totally consistent with your free will as a free spirit, and that there's never any interference with that free will; and that you are, in fact, unconditional love and, as you let yourself feel that, you accept and love yourself more, and you feel yourself supported in every way by the universal love with the result that you have access to whatever you need by way of wisdom, knowledge, material things, love, and that you are flowing comprehensively with life and with the totality of consciousness.

As you progress with that exercise, which I suggest should be done daily, you will find that a certain suspension of thought takes place for a little while which allows you to become absorbed in the feeling of what you are and your place in the cosmic scheme of things. This, in turn, leaves you open to new patterns of thought and to give more and more expression to your higher self, or oversoul, as I prefer to call it.

The exercise, in itself, helps you to accept and integrate yourself. It also gives you free and unlimited access to universal energy or love. Remember that it's all about feeling, or, more accurately, letting go into feeling; included in that letting go are your conditioned, rational, thought processes.

I suggest that you extend the exercise to include in the circle (through imagination, of course) any person to whom you wish to send love, or any situation about which you are concerned, and, in general, all the souls in the universe, both in physical bodies and in spirit.

As you sit/stand in your imaginary circle and let yourself flow with the feelings of love, it is impossible for you to have any realistic concept of the value of what you are doing in the context of the raising of consciousness, individually, where the sending of love to a particular soul or souls is concerned, and universally, through the spreading of love around every soul in the universe. Yet I can tell you categorically that if only one person in a thousand were doing that exercise, or something similar, on a regular, (e.g., daily), basis the effect would be so powerful that within a relatively short time span in your terms, say, about fifty years, there would be no wars, no crime, the freedom of the individual would be respected, and planet earth would be a wonderfully harmonious place, with the result that the way back to full awareness would be immeasurably so much shorter and less painful.

It is important to realise that it may take a considerable length of time for a deeply divided personality to be ready to receive help. (Looking for or needing help, and being ready to receive it, are two vastly different things, unfortunately.) That's why I recommended (in our last session) the approach of becoming as a child; children are more ready than adults to receive help.

What else can you do to help? Be patient and wait for an opportunity to present itself. How will you recognise the opportunity? If you trust yourself enough, you will. Trying to be helpful, even with the highest motivation, causes more problems than almost anything else when the person apparently needing help is not ready to receive it. As always, you won't be surprised when I tell you that the ideal thing to do – after, needless to say (!), you have done the exercise I recommended earlier – is to hand the whole situation over to your guides and then flow with whatever presents itself.

The sceptic may say that I haven't offered any practical solution, something concrete that one can hold on to, something to do, as distinct from sitting around, feeling and thinking and letting go. What I'm trying to convey is that doing, as commonly understood, is often not doing, or undoing, a reinforcement of the negative, or subconscious (within my meaning of the word 'subconscious'). The only reality is internal. What human beings tend to see as reality is a passing parade of events and things and even human existence which are replaced and remembered or forgotten like yesterday or last week or last month or last year. So, if you don't internalise your reality, – or, I should say, accept that your reality is internal – it is impossible for you to be yourself; you are mainly living your life as a puppet or an automaton, however successful you may seem to be to outward appearances. The doing follows automatically and at the best times when the (internal) reality is created and accepted.

THE ATLANTEAN EXPERIMENT

20th June, 1989 – 15th February, 1992: I thought we might give a little time to talking about Atlantis regarding which there has been a good deal of speculation, including as to whether it existed at all. There was such a place. In terms of your time it ceased to exist some 400,000 years ago.

While Atlantis was a land mass it was different from the earth as you know it. Atlanteans were not human as you are. They were, of course, spirit beings like you, but their bodies were not dense like yours.

Atlantis was an experiment which, if it had worked, would have shortened considerably the journey back to full awareness. It was designed as a model and a basis for a more extended form of evolution. There were about a hundred million souls altogether involved in the experiment, which lasted for a period of about 50,000 years.

It would, I think, be fair to describe the Atlantean experiment as a halfway state between life in spirit and life on earth, as you know it. As I have said, Atlantis was a land mass, but it did not have vegetation such as the earth now has. Neither did it initially have animal life, but experimentation with animal, including bird, life was subsequently introduced. The idea was that it would be inhabited by souls who had reached a fairly advanced stage of evolution and who would be subjected to some limitation of power by taking on bodies. In appearance the bodies were somewhat like your bodies, but there were no deformities, or colour distinctions. They were male and female. They did not need food in order to survive, nor did they need transport in order to get from place to place; as in spirit, creation, including movement, was achieved through thought. Yet, both the land and the bodies had substance, in the material sense of the word.

Atlantis was designed as a learning experience in a transitional way and there was no question of it being more than that. Ultimately, its undoing was that the old power hunger began to take over and some souls started a process of confusing appearance with reality; for example, they thought that immortality was attainable in Atlantis. They (rightly) concluded that life was energy, so they looked at sources of apparently ever-continuing energy, such as the sun. So why not tap that energy, focus it and transfer it into their bodies? Much experimentation was carried out in that field, with crystals being the most common focal points. There was, and could be, only temporary success. Their mistake was that they did not understand that they were spirit beings, a combination of feelings and thoughts merging into consciousness, who did not need any external trappings, such as physical bodies, to achieve immortality. They were, of course, already immortal, but either were not aware of that or wanted immortality within the conditions which they had created for themselves in Atlantis. (The search for physical immortality has continued through subsequent civilisations and, indeed, the doctrine of the resurrection of the body on "the last day", which is enshrined in some religious belief systems, stems from that search.)

All souls, as spirit beings, have unlimited power. In their ultimate state of total awareness they use that power with complete respect for each and every other soul. All the pain and trauma of the fall from awareness and the journey back to awareness have resulted from the abuse of power. Atlantis was designed as a vehicle for increasing awareness through limitation of power, which would have the effect that souls would have to learn to interact with, and relate to, each other with respect and co-operation. As things turned out, the Atlantean situation was not restrictive enough. The souls taking part in the experiment remembered too much of their spirit state and the demonstration of what might loosely be termed magic/psychic tricks – in other words, external manifestation of power – became an end in itself.

What happened to Atlantis? It was a democracy with its own

government, which consisted of a council of representatives selected by the people. In theory, the council was subject to periodic change. In practice, that did not happen in that, within a relatively short period of time, there was a distinct ruling class, which began to revel more and more in the trappings of power.

Tyranny breeds rebellion. The free spirit does not want to be caged. So, as the rulers became more autocratic, counter movements started. Conflict, repression, isolation, cruelty, violent deaths, all the things that are so familiar to your world, followed. Inevitably, what started out as an idealistic revolution turned into a power struggle, with both sides becoming equally obsessed with the use (abuse) of power – although, of course, they would have recoiled from the idea that they were bedfellows. In any event, it became clear with the passage of time that Atlantis was a doomed civilisation. The grand designers felt that developments were too closely following the pattern of the earlier fall from awareness and decided that a fresh start with a more limited human expression was desirable. Accordingly, Atlantis was allowed to "self-destruct", which was the inevitable result of its own advanced knowledge combined with power obsession. For the modem equivalent, you have only to consider two superpowers competing for world domination, with technology capable of achieving unlimited destruction available to both of them. When each side wanted to dominate the other and each side was convinced of its own invincibility, then there could only be one outcome, given the capacity for destruction available to both sides. So Atlantis literally destroyed itself.

Most of the former inhabitants of Atlantis are at present on earth and are to the forefront in advanced consciousness growth areas. In the evolutionary process which they have undergone since Atlantis they have to a large extent learned the lessons posed by the Atlantean experience.

Earth, as you know it, was deliberately designed as a more restrictive experience so that access to power would be less easily attainable. Nonetheless, the pursuit of power has been obsessive for many people – and not only the people who have achieved notoriety. The obsession has operated, and continues to operate in the interaction of personal relationships and, perhaps most insidiously, in the intimacy of one-to-one relationships.

The purpose of the Atlantean experiment, as it is the purpose of planet earth as it now exists, was to help souls to shed the mud of unawareness. As I have already said, Atlantis was intended as a model which could be expanded upon. It failed as a model but not as an experiment in that the design of a more restrictive form of earth life which would, it was hoped, enable progress to be made more surely, if more slowly, followed from it. The stage has now been reached on planet earth, of course, that, technologically, it has the capacity to destroy itself, or, rather, be destroyed by opposing forces. However, as I have said in an earlier session, I don't foresee that happening.

My main purpose in this session is to focus on growth of awareness, or enlightenment, which is a commonly-used word in this context. Souls would have been saved much pain if the Atlantean model had worked as a model. It didn't work because essentially enlightenment came to be equated with power. A miracle worker is an obvious example of somebody who has power. Does it automatically follow that the miracle worker is enlightened? If not, from where does he derive his power?

Many evolved souls have, through the centuries, come to earth and performed miracles; in other words, they have achieved results which are not normally possible within the limits of human endeavour. What feats have come to be classified as miracles were commonplace in Atlantis. All the earth miracle workers were (are) former Atlanteans. They were (are) not necessarily more enlightened than many other souls whose life purposes were (are) fulfilled in obscurity. They have recognised (as other non-miracle workers also have) that physical manifestation is ultimately an illusion and that spirit life is the only reality. This recognition enabled (enables) them to transcend the normal limitations of earth. They simply have not accepted (do not accept) those limitations.

At the same time, no human being has ever been able to perform what you would classify as a miracle without the aid of spirit helpers. At different times it has served the purpose of the grand design that miracles should be performed and the agent to fulfil that purpose has agreed to be born into earth. It is, and always has been, a delicate mission. The agent is placed in a powerful position and needs to have evolved into a deep and permanent sense of his own reality as a part of God, equal to, but no better than, every other part, if he is to escape the recurring trap of power (egotism).

As his awareness grows, or, more accurately, as his unawareness diminishes, the spiritual traveller will be more and more conscious that he has access to all the evolved energy of the universe but that that consciousness does not give him any right to set himself above others or to exert dominion over them. Accordingly, he will not seek to set himself up as a guru, or a cult figure. In saying that, I don't mean to make any judgement on personalities who, during the course of the earth's evolution, have become cult figures and some of whom have had profound influence on the pattern of that evolution. There's a world of difference between seeking pre-eminence and having it attributed to you. Souls cannot avoid sharing what they are. They do so either negatively or positively, in a limited way or widely. The more they accept themselves for what they are, the extent of their sharing of themselves inevitably widens. They are "ordinary" souls in the sense that they are equal (in God) with all other souls, but they are extraordinary human beings – which may often be a source of confusion until one accepts the transitional and illusory nature of humanity.

THE BIBLE

6th June, 1988 – 26th October, 1992: The Bible has everything known to the human condition; for example, devotion, power, mystery, grandeur, anger, judgement, lust, war, peace, pestilence, plagues, miracles, faith, hope, charity, cruelty, compassion, ruthlessness, destruction, birth, death, sickness, incest, rape, pillage, righteousness, intolerance, tolerance, greed, envy, insecurity, sacrifice, beauty, ugliness, fear, love.

By and large, the Old Testament is a story of harshness with an emphasis on fear, while the New Testament stresses compassion and love.

How did the Bible come to be written? Was it divinely inspired? How historically accurate is it?

The Bible was the product of many minds, some in spirit, some in physical bodies. The various parts of it were written over a long period of time and through different incarnations. Some souls worked on it both in spirit and in repeated physical incarnations; for example, Matthew, Mark, Luke and John, who later wrote the four Gospels of the New Testament, had earlier participated in the writing of the Old Testament. The various contributors set down the material as it came to them and did not envisage it forming part of a best-selling book. Others later combined to bring all the parts together, and the Bible as you know it came into being. The original writings were much transformed in the process by editing, re-editing and translation. Changes were made in order to make the writings conform with current beliefs. The four Gospels, in particular, were subject to substantial editing, both to fit in with desired beliefs and to make them consistent with each other as far as possible.

Since everything is the work of God, since each soul is divine, the Bible was, of course, divinely inspired. Much of it is allegorical. The Old Testament should be seen in that way and not as a historical document. Yet there is a factual thread running through it. The evolution into the human state did start with two people. The models were already there from the first stage (as described in our first book). Adam and Eve, as the two people have been called, did exist. As a matter of interest, Eve's body was not formed out of one of Adam's ribs but was created in its own right as the female model for the human race. All the other characters mentioned in the Old Testament also existed.

The description of Adam and Eve being banished from the Garden of Eden is highly dramatic. It represents in a physically understandable way what the fall from awareness meant. The temptation of power, then the nakedness of unawareness and the struggle to get back to the former state are all there once one looks beyond the literal representation. Similarly, the story of Cain and Abel, although they also existed, is dramatised to highlight the duality of the unaware state.

As we have already seen, life on earth was designed to help souls find their way back to their former state of full awareness. The process of evolutionary growth, which we have called the grand design, started through various forms of non-human life, and at a certain stage the time was ripe, in a manner of speaking, for the creation of the human species with the capacity to exercise free will. The evolution of the human race could ideally be likened to the growth of a child through adolescence to adulthood (and wisdom!). In the early stages (childhood) a lot of discipline (regulation) is necessary, even to ensure survival. Thus, the Old Testament shows the Father repeatedly instructing the child, even to the extent of handing down Commandments. The emphasis on love in the New Testament mirrors the expected growth in consciousness as the child reaches adulthood. Now he has the key to the door – which is love; a simple, positive message.

You want to know about Sodom and Gomorrah; and the Flood.

The Biblical version is that the inhabitants of Sodom and Gomorrah had reached such a level of depravity that God decided to send two angels to warn them that they would be destroyed if they did not change their ways; that only one man, Lot, listened to the angels; that because nobody else heeded the warning Lot agreed to take his family away to safety; that, as they left, he and his wife and two daughters were warned not to look backwards; that his poor wife, presumably overcome by curiosity, yielded to the temptation to look back and was immediately turned into a pillar of salt; and that Sodom and Gomorrah and all their inhabitants were destroyed by fire and brimstone.

In the telling of the story the moral took precedence over the facts. Sodom and Gomorrah existed. Though they were described as cities they were only small communities or towns compared with what would be described as cities today. The biblical version clearly indicates that the "sin" of the inhabitants of Sodom and Gomorrah was homosexuality; it is stated that the male inhabitants came to Lot's house and tried to get the angels (who were male) to come out so that they could have "sex" with them. Lot is reported to have pleaded with them to take his two daughters instead (which doesn't say much for the value placed on women's status at the time!). His offer was, apparently, not accepted, but the angels succeeded in getting Lot and his daughters safely away before the fire and brimstone descended.

So what did happen? If you substitute Abraham for God you have the key to the story – and, of course, Abraham was (is) God in the sense that every soul is. Many complaints had been made to Abraham, who was Lot's uncle and who was accepted as a type of patriarchal overlord of the region, about the behaviour of the inhabitants of Sodom and Gomorrah. He yielded to pressure and sent two representatives (angels – as all souls) to warn them that he would destroy them and all their possessions if they didn't change their ways. They didn't listen and the representatives set fire to the towns while the people were sleeping. Lot's wife strenuously objected to leaving. She wept copiously (pillar of salt!), lay on the ground and refused to move. She literally died of a broken heart.

The happening of Sodom and Gomorrah has been repeated many times over throughout the history of the world. Countless acts of destruction have been carried out by "righteous" people in the name of God. How many children – and adults – have been terrorised by being threatened with God's anger and eternal punishment (fire again!) if they didn't behave themselves according to God's rules – interpreted, of course, by God fearing people!

In fairness to Abraham, one of the considerations influencing him, apart from righteousness, was that continuation or extension of the practices of the inhabitants of Sodom and Gomorrah would jeopardise the survival of the human race.

According to Genesis, and, indeed, historically, Noah lived long before Abraham. Noah is mostly remembered as the man who, with his family and selected animals, survived in a specially-designed ark the great flood which destroyed all other life on earth. The biblical version, if taken literally, is a horrific story of a wrathful, unmerciful God inflicting destruction on the scale of a nuclear holocaust in modern times. But, of course, that couldn't have happened since such a God didn't – and doesn't – exist. What really happened was that there was a flood which was confined to the particular part of the world in which Noah lived. For the chroniclers of the Bible that was all the world; in those days of restricted communication the extent of the world was very limited as far as those living in it were concerned. Noah had the foresight to be well prepared. The story is accurate within its own terms once the limits of the world within the knowledge and vision of the tellers are recognised. It doesn't take much of a leap of the imagination to ascribe such an apparently enormous disaster to a wrathful God, and to see Noah as specially singled out and favoured by God. Even today, what are regarded as disasters, e.g., Aids, are often described as, and believed to be, punishment by God for misbehaviour. And it doesn't have to be a major disaster; plaintive cries, such as, "What did I do wrong? Why am I being punished like this?" are commonplace responses to everyday happenings.

The Bible is really an account of the human experiment up to a certain stage, with all its struggles and traumas and coming to terms with its freedom of expression. It is not an objective account; all the contributors to it to a greater or lesser extent directed their efforts subjectively according to their own points of view, or the points of view which they deemed to be required of them. It is also (understandably) selective. For example, the real Jesus was different in many respects from the Jesus portrayed in the Gospels. One of the most striking things about Jesus was his sense of humour. The pietistic and somewhat punitive, albeit compassionate, representation of him in the Gospels emerged from the editing and re-editing processes and were in line with the thinking of an organisation which was constantly extending its power base; love and humour are not seen as effective methods of control. In fairness to the chroniclers, though, most of the sentiments attributed to him were expressed by Jesus and the words used convey those sentiments accurately enough, although, of course, he said and did many things which are not recorded and which, if they had been, would have given a much more rounded picture of him. He was a compassionate, loving, humorous man, who was hot-tempered and often impatient, especially in his earlier years. He was much more relaxed in himself by the time he came to fulfil his public mission as Jesus. The last thing he wanted was to be put on a pedestal and adored. His aim was to bring people with him, not to set himself apart from them. If he were not so aware of the grand design he would have found it difficult to endure all the suffering that has been caused in his name. However, he realises that he was a catalyst, a harbinger of changing consciousness, and he is happy about that.

If you look up John's Gospel you will see that Jesus is recorded as telling his disciples about a comforter/counsellor who would be sent by the Father "to be with you for ever", "to teach you all things". He was, of course, talking about the grand design, the process by which souls from what I have categorised as the fourth stage of evolutionary growth act as guides or guardian angels for those souls who are still struggling along the path of increasing awareness.

There's nothing new, really, in what I'm communicating to you. I'm putting somewhat differently and from a new perspective (and more simply, I hope) what has been transmitted by many others through the centuries. An aspect of the earth experience is that mystique – like dust! – increases with the passage of time if it isn't cleared away. So, you can think of me – and, maybe, yourself? – as a duster – which, if you like it, could be a particularly appropriate title for you, since you have been wondering what you should call yourself!

HIGHER SELF/OVERSOUL/GUIDES?

16th March, 1992: People sometimes seem to find difficulty in reconciling the concept of guides with that of the higher self or the oversoul. And, indeed, are the higher self and the oversoul one and the same thing?

The oversoul is the total you. It sends out an aspect of itself – the soul – to increase its bank of awareness. As (if) the soul grows in consciousness during its earth life it integrates itself more and more with the oversoul, which, in my terminology, is the higher self. (Incidentally, I don't like the description "higher self" as, in its usage, it implies the existence of a lower self. The self is, of its nature, divine and, therefore, does not lend itself to categorisation into higher or lower definitions; accordingly, I prefer to use the word "oversoul".) There is never total integration during an earth lifetime, although some souls – rare exceptions – have come a long way towards it. The physical body wouldn't be able to cope with the full energy of the oversoul.

The function of guides (guardian angels) is to help the soul to integrate as far as possible with the oversoul. Guides don't give instructions or directions – their role is to guide, not command. The giving of instructions or directions in the sense of mandatory commands would, in any case, be an interference with free will. The guides give guidance to those who are open to receive it in order to help them along the path of increasing awareness. The guidance tends to become more subtle and less straightforward as awareness increases.

There has never been, nor is there now, any person on earth, no matter how evolved, who did not, or does not, need help. Each person begins life as a child, with total dependence for survival on another or others; and all through its life on earth that person has to be helped in different ways by many people. The giving and receiving of help are so much a feature of the daily routine of life that they don't need any comment, other than that payment for services rendered often obscures the fact that both the services and the payment are part of the processes of giving and receiving help.

It stands to reason that if people need so much help with the physical aspects of life they also need help with the non-physical, or spiritual aspects. Guides are there to help with all aspects of life. They make the process easier. Souls have free will. They don't have to have guides to help them; but their journeys back to full awareness will be longer and more painful if they don't allow themselves to be helped along the way. The grand design was framed as a vast co-operative effort with souls at higher levels of awareness helping those at lower levels, subject, of course, to their being willing to receive help.

The oversoul in its ultimate (former) state of full awareness has access to the totality of (divine) consciousness. It is that consciousness, but, of course, is not all of it. We have discussed the relationship of the individual soul/oversoul to God/love/feeling and all its expressions in previous sessions, and I don't think there's any need to go into all that again. What I want to bring to attention in this session is that, in the case of people who are still working through earth lifetimes, the oversouls have not yet reached – or, I should say, regained – total awareness and, therefore, still need help in the development of their relationship (a) with themselves and (b) with God/love/feeling and all its expressions.

My approach is basically uncomplicated: if there's a choice between a simple and a difficult way of achieving the same result, choose the simple way. If you have luggage to carry, it's much easier to let it be carried for you by whatever mechanical means are available to you than to carry it on your back. Your guides will help to relieve you of the burden of unawareness if you allow them to do so. Then you will find yourself – you as oversoul in fullness of awareness – sooner. It's always nice to find something you lost, isn't it? – not to mention something as valuable as yourself!

If you keep in mind the simplicity of no separation, unity – God is all, all is God, we are all in God – you will find that the complexities of compartmentalisation – guides, higher self, oversoul, etc. – fade away. Then it will be easier to allow all the evolved energy of the universe to support you in every way.

TIME AND SPACE

6th June – 25th July: You've been questioning where our sessions are going from here. Have we covered everything? If people can get to the stage of being divine consciousness and acting out of that feeling, isn't that the last word? Would saying any more only lead to repetition and confusion?

How about looking a little further at the notion of time and space? Yes, we've touched on that before and explained that time and space, as you know them, are a feature of earth only. In the world of spirit there's no time or space, just continually evolving consciousness. You know the feeling of time standing still when you're totally absorbed in, say, a pleasurable experience and you're free of any pressure of having to be somewhere or meet somebody at a particular time. That's the nearest I can get to an analogy which may make the idea of existing within a timeless and spaceless experience understandable to you.

Over and over in our sessions the aim of unity – no separation - is fostered, Why, then, did the grand design make things so apparently complicated by having different systems in operation in the worlds of spirit and earth when the purpose of life on earth seems to be to bring the two together so that earth is ideally an aid to the spiritual? Death is the answer.

The death of physical life allows transition and growth with the possibility of fresh starts. The linear time and space framework enables an ageing process – which is not a feature of non-physical life. Thus the body deteriorates and eventually gives up and the soul is then in a position to have a look at how it evolved during its earth life; and, if it seems desirable to do so, it can, in due course, decide to have another try without burdening itself with conscious memories of past attempts.

Earth is an illusion in the sense that, in eternal terms, it has no reality. It provides a platform for physical happenings – such as, birth, growth, varying experiences in between birth and death – but the happenings pass and are only important ultimately in the effects they create. The soul exists, and continues to exist, whether within a physical cage or out of it, and expresses itself through its feelings and thoughts, which is how it creates its reality, its own universe. Ultimately, then, feelings and thoughts are the only reality. We are our feelings and thoughts. Thus there's no physical limitation to us, we don't age, we don't die, we just evolve in consciousness. Time and space are a measurement of limitation which only applies to physical bodies and the physical environment.

A big challenge, which is coming more into focus at present, is how to merge the timeless and spaceless dimension of spirit with the time and space framework of earth. One of the factors that made progress in the earth experiment so painfully slow has been that expression of spirituality has, particularly through religious culture, tended to imply rejection of the physical or material, including, often, the physical body and its functioning. Sacrifice, penance, self-denial, led to holiness, which was the ideal objective of spiritual searching. Because of the lack of understanding of the continuity of life and, within that, the purpose of life on earth, it didn't register that rejection of the physical made nonsense of being born into earth. Life on earth has no point if the physical world, including, of course, physical bodies, is not seen as an aid to the spiritual and not as something separate from it. A soul which rejects its physical body is negating its opportunity for growth through earth experience and might as well not have bothered coming into earth at all.

Yet, rejection of the physical in pursuit of the spiritual has had its own logic. By withdrawing from the physical and transcending it one could free oneself from its limitations – which tend to be reinforced by time and space. One could enter into a meditative state where time would cease to have any meaning and where all the day-to-day problems of life fade into insignificance and where even eating for survival becomes largely irrelevant. The difficulty, as I see it, with that approach is that it is essentially an avoidance of the earth experience and that's why so many souls who have followed that path in previous lives are now extending their search into the hurly-burly of daily participative living on earth – and are not finding that easy. They tend to find the pull of "getting away from it all" particularly strong.

So – trying to reach more into the timeless and space less dimension of spirit by running away from the time and space framework of earth doesn't work in the long run. "I have no time for myself, ... I have no space . . . . . I need to get away . . . . . I need to be somewhere where there are no people making demands on me . . . . . no telephones . . . . . no clocks . . . . . no contact with all the problems of life . . . . ." and so on – these are familiar expressions of response to pressures of time and space. People are stressed because of their work, or because they have no work, they haven't enough time, or they have time on their hands, or because they are in confining, difficult relationships or situations and sometimes the most desirable, if extreme, solution seems to be to end it all, to escape into a hoped for oblivion of nothingness. But, in reality, there's no escape. Any new relationship or situation will bring the old with it because, ultimately, it's a matter of consciousness expressed through feelings and thoughts. Time and space are irrelevant where consciousness is concerned. It exists outside of them and is the continuing link between the world of spirit and the world of earth, so that, in fact, they are all one. As one reaches that awareness there's no longer any relevance in the idea of getting away from it all, because the "it all" is internal.

In practical terms, then, how does it work? How does a human being meet the challenge of merging the timeless and space less dimension of spirit with the time and space framework of earth? Firstly, by accepting that he is a soul, a spirit being, temporarily using a physical body, and that souls do not age nor are they confined by space; and, secondly, by realising and accepting that the soul expresses itself through its feelings and thoughts and that, therefore, all the happenings of the earth experience are only important in the effects they create on those feelings and thoughts.

All that does not mean that a person will not, or should not, participate fully in the human experience. In fact, through that acceptance he will find much greater freedom in participating in, and enjoying, the experience of earth. His awareness will be expanded. He won't assume limitations of time, such as ageing, or space, such as location. In short, he will be able to call himself a free spirit and know that he is truly so. He will understand and accept that governmental systems, religions, social conventions, are all just transitional ways of ordering and controlling behavioural patterns, and he can be totally free of them while ostensibly living in conformity with them, if he so wishes. He will not allow himself to be boxed in, to be categorised, to be labelled, to be limited by definition. He will play the game according to its rules, but he will know that it's only a game. In the true spirit of the game he will know that it's how he will participate in it that's important.

Just as he will not allow himself to be categorised, etc., equally, he will not categorise others. By granting himself freedom, he also extends it to all others, without exception. No longer will he judge himself, no longer will he judge others. There's no yardstick for judgement when there are no definitions. The boundaries are gone, there's no time or space, the spirit is free to be, to express itself as it is, it reaches out to hug and embrace the whole universe with all the warmth, the joy, the simplicity, the comprehensive and glorious infinity of its unconditional love.

UNCONDITIONAL LOVE

28th December 1991 – 10th November 1992: We have referred to unconditional love at different times during our sessions. What is unconditional love? How can one practise it? Better still, how can one be it?

The word *unconditional* means, of course, without conditions, no hooks, no ifs or buts. We have already considered love in detail and have described it – I hope less ambiguously – as feeling and all its expressions, which includes both aware and unaware expressions and which otherwise I have divided into feeling and emotion, with feeling being the aware expression of love and emotion being the unaware expression.

Love, then, is unlimited expression of feeling in all its manifestations. Unconditional love is unlimited acceptance of feeling in all its manifestations; in other words, whatever the expression is – tolerance, rejection, compassion, resentment, positive or negative – love accepts it as it is, without judgement.

The crunch question is – how does it work in practice? Using the word you in a general way instead of the more impersonal word *one*, I'll explore the question as best I can.

Suppose you are a parent. Do you expect your son/daughter to behave in certain ways, to conform with certain traditions or social mores? For instance, if they are drug addicts do you accept them? Or sexually promiscuous? Or in an 'illicit' relationship? Or 'gay'? Or resentful of you? Or uncommunicative with you?

If you don't accept them as they are, you are not being

unconditionally loving.

Suppose you are a partner in an intimate relationship, such as marriage. If you find that your partner is having, or has had, an affair with somebody else, how do you feel? Rejected? Hurt? Resentful? Angry? Hating? Did you feel that you loved your partner before you found out about the affair? Has that love now changed to hatred? If so, what was the nature of the love? If you love unconditionally, does that love not remain constant in spite of what your partner may do or have done? If it does not remain constant, it is not unconditional love.

These are but two examples. Others would, of course, also apply, such as, relationships within families generally, with friends and acquaintances, with neighbours, in work situations.

If you love unconditionally, then, does that mean that you allow yourself to be treated in any old way, to be just a doormat? Not at all. As we have seen, unconditional love means acceptance of people and situations as they are, without judgement. That doesn't mean that you have to like the people (or aspects of them), or the situations, or that you don't want them to change.

As always, everything — your world — starts with yourself. It is impossible for you to love others unconditionally if you don't love yourself unconditionally. In unconditional, loving, acceptance of yourself it is impossible for you not to have respect for yourself and in such a way that it is impossible for anybody else to undermine that respect.

So, what happens? What do you do? In the first example given above do you say to your son/daughter – 'Yes, it's fine with me that you're a drug addict, or sexually promiscuous, or whatever'? Or, in the second example do you say to your partner – 'I don't mind that you're having, or have had, an affair'? No, unconditional love does not demand those kinds of responses. In my view, the type of response that would be consistent with unconditional love would be something like this – 'I love you, but I don't like certain things about you, the way you're behaving.' You're expressing your position, the way you feel. You're not imposing conditions on the other person, e.g., 'I love you, but I can't continue to love you unless you change your behaviour in the following ways.' You're leaving it open to the other person to change his behaviour, or not, as he wishes. You're also leaving it open to yourself as to how you'll respond to the change, or no change, as the case may be.

The most difficult challenges to unconditional love come, I think, in the area of intimate, e.g., marital-type, relationships, since those relationships are particularly subject to intense emotions, such as, jealousy, possessiveness, hurt, rejection. Such relationships present wonderful opportunities for growth in awareness. Accordingly, it would be helpful, I hope, to go a little further with the second example – where, say, your partner is having an affair with somebody else. Let's assume you have expressed your feelings about it along the lines outlined above. Suppose your partner is not willing to make any change in his behaviour. You wouldn't be human if you didn't feel hurt, rejected, resentful, angry. How do you cope with those emotions? How can you transform them into unconditional love? And then, consistent with unconditional love, what do you do?

First things first – you start with yourself. In loving yourself unconditionally you accept yourself as you are, which means acknowledging your emotions. That acknowledgement helps you to deal with them more easily. You understand that those emotions may actually be helpful to you temporarily but that, in the long run, they can only damage you spiritually. You allow yourself to experience hurt, resentment, etc., but you understand that the real you, the soul/divine you, is not emotional, cannot, in fact, be hurt, or resentful, or rejected; so that, once you have acknowledged your emotions and given yourself some latitude with them, the best way to free yourself from them is to let them go into the divine you, or hand them over to your guides, which is, in effect, the same thing. The more you can let go, the more your consciousness merges with the divine consciousness, which, of course, is free from emotions.

And, then, what do you do? Do you decide to stay with your partner or separate from him? If you stay, what form does your relationship take? For instance, if he wishes to maintain his relationship with you while at the same time keeping his affair going, do you continue to have sexual intercourse with him? The simple answer to all the questions is that with the freedom of unconditional love you do whatever you want to do. All the factors which would prevent you from truly expressing your own feelings have been removed.

Yes, but, you argue, suppose you have young children and are financially dependent on him, having, perhaps, given up your own career in order to take care of the children, and suppose you want to have nothing more to do with him, how, then, can you do what you want to do? If you are truly loving unconditionally, or, more accurately, being unconditional love, that question will never arise. A solution to enable you to do what you want will present itself. That's the way the loving energy of the universe, of God, works. There's no element of chance in it: it's as inevitable as night following day, or day following night. It's the unfailing way of the universe.

An unavoidable conclusion from what I'm saying is that, if you're in a situation that irks you, that you find intolerable in some way, or even simply that you don't like, it's a sure indication that you're not loving unconditionally. In that case, unless, of course, you want to stay in the situation as it is, I suggest that you look at it, determine what it is about it that you find intolerable, or that you don't like, and then hand it over unconditionally to your guides, divine consciousness, the God within, whichever is most comfortable for you. If you allow yourself to trust in the process with no reservations, no conditions, I promise you that the outcome will be a source of wonder and of joy to you.

As I have stressed repeatedly in our sessions, life on earth is a platform for growth in consciousness. It is not a law of the universe that growth has to be a painful process. In practice, it has been so. Conditioned thinking has tended to isolate humanity into a prison of spirituality or spiritual growth being achieved through self-denial, self-sacrifice, suffering. Once that belief system is allowed to prevail, that's the only way that growth can occur. I cannot emphasise enough that there's another way, a better way. Love does not demand pain and suffering. Enjoyment is central to love. Life on earth is intended to be an enjoyable experience. If that statement sounds in any way frivolous to you, please examine it. How do you enjoy yourself? Through self-expression; being how you like to be; doing what you like to do. And I'm sure you'll agree that ultimately your enjoyment comes from relating to people in the most loving possible way.

UNCONDITIONAL LOVE (CONTINUED)

16th November: Arising out of the last session, you ask how does one know if one has handed over a situation unconditionally.

I suggest that you ask yourself the following questions:
In the handing over process
a) are you looking for a specified outcome?;
b) are you looking for an outcome within a particular time limit?;
c) are you saying to yourself that because you've been doing everything "right" life owes you what you would consider a favourable outcome?;
d) are you stipulating that you won't be able to get on with your work of, say, service to humanity unless your situation changes in a particular way?;
e) are you leaving the outcome completely open, knowing that, whatever it is, it will bring the best possible solution to your situation *in a way which you will find not only enjoyable but better than anything you could have envisaged?*

If the answers to any or all of the questions (a) to (d) are' yes', then you know that the process is still conditional as far as you are concerned. If you can give a positive answer to (e), then your handing over is unconditional.

So, then, you have handed over (or turned over, if you like) unconditionally. What next? You still have to go on living your life. How does the solution happen? You are, of course, a participant in the emergence of a solution. You literally 'go with the flow', follow your feelings, do whatever feels best to you, constantly reminding yourself of your unconditional handing over of the situation. Life is never stagnant. There's nothing passive about the handing over process. It means aligning yourself with all the evolved energy of the universe in fulfilling your life purpose.

CONCLUSION

28th December: The fact that the recording of the material in this book has taken much longer than was the case with our first two books seems to me to be a good reason for having ended this book on a note of unconditional love!

Whatever length of time it takes, realisation of a state of unconditional love is the ultimate objective of all souls reaching towards the regaining of full awareness.

ABOUT THE AUTHOR

Paddy McMahon was born in 1933 in County Clare in the west of Ireland, and has lived in Dublin since 1952. Employed in the Irish Civil Service from 1952 until 1988, he became aware that he and all people had spirit guides-guardian angels, and that we can communicate with them if we so choose. These communications began in 1978, and inspired him to become increasingly involved in spiritual counseling and lecturing. Paddy's first communications from the highly-evolved spiritual being Shebaka began in 1981.

BOOKS BY PADDY MCMAHON

There Are No Goodbyes:
Guided By Angels - My Tour of the Spirit World

Peacemonger:
More Dialogue with Margaret Anna Cusack

Living without Fear:
Dialogue with J. Krishnamurti

Amongst Equals:
More Dialogue with J. Krishnamurti

A Free Spirit:
Dialogue with Margaret Anna Cusack The Nun of Kenmare

The Joy of Being
Illustrations by Michel

The Grand Design:
Reflections of a soul / oversoul
Selected excerpts from the five volumes

The Grand Design – V:
Reflections of a soul / oversoul

The Grand Design – IV:
Reflections of a soul / oversoul

The Grand Design – III:
Reflections of a soul / oversoul

The Grand Design – II:
Reflections of a soul / oversoul

The Grand Design – I:
Reflections of a soul / oversoul

Printed in Great Britain
by Amazon

74436916R00058